THE JOHN F. KENNEDY
SCHOOL OF GOVERNMENT

8/9

The John F. Kennedy School of Government

THE FIRST FIFTY YEARS

Prepared by
The John F. Kennedy School of Government

50

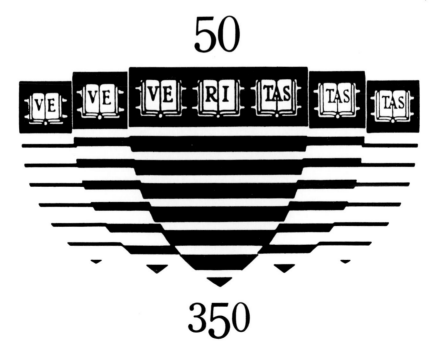

350

BALLINGER PUBLISHING COMPANY
Cambridge, Massachusetts
A SUBSIDIARY OF HARPER & ROW, PUBLISHERS, INC.

International Standard Book Number: 0-88730-138-X

Library of Congress Catalog Card Number: 86-14030

Printed in the United States of America
Designed by Copenhaver Cumpston

Library of Congress Cataloging-in-Publication Data

The John F. Kennedy School of Government.

    Includes index.
    1. John F. Kennedy School of Government—History.
I. John F. Kennedy School of Government.
JF1338.J64J64   1986   350'.0007'1174461   86-14030
ISBN 0-88730-138-X

Contents

Acknowledgments

Success does indeed have a thousand fathers. I would like to recognize, with sincere appreciation, those whose loyalty and commitment to this School have made this history possible.

Don K. Price proposed the idea that this history be written. Steven L. Rearden prepared the original text. Professor Ernest R. May revised and edited the text with assistance from other "survivors" including David Bell, John T. Dunlop, Oscar Handlin, Edward Mason, John Montgomery, Jonathan Moore, Richard Neustadt, W. Scott Payne, Don K. Price, Howard Raiffa, and others. Research assistants Douglas Strand and Jonathan Marshall helped track down and sort out the facts from the fiction. Malcolm Hamilton, the Kennedy School's librarian, rose to the occasion and served as our "archivist"—which meant creating archives for us that previously had not existed. Shirley Brooks, whose own tenure as secretary to Dean Don K. Price, helped Malcolm in building the archives. Finally, Heather Pars Campion, coordinator for the School's 50th Anniversary Celebration, also coordinated this project with efficiency, humor, and grace.

Graham Allison
April 1986

THE JOHN F. KENNEDY
SCHOOL OF GOVERNMENT

The John F. Kennedy School of Government Today

Fifty years ago Harvard had no special school for government. But then, eighty years ago it had no school for business; until the nineteenth century, none for law; until the eighteenth century, none for medicine. As President Derek Bok explained at the dedication of the new Littauer Center in 1978:

. . . [D]espite the difficulty of the issues our leaders face, despite the difficulty of managing our public institutions, we have not had a tradition of serious, careful preparation for positions of public leadership comparable to the preparation provided for those entering our great private professions. That is the *principal missing link* in American higher education today.[1]

In attempting to provide that missing link in American higher education today, the School seeks to hold up the highest standards for public service and to attract the best possible talent to government and public problem-solving. The "profession" of government—career, appointed, or elected—is not one in which a professional school certifies competence for entry, as schools of medicine and law have come to do. In this sense, government is more like business and the Kennedy School more like the Business School. The public sector is disorganized and likely to remain so. At least in the American setting, this disorganization reflects a deep ambivalence about government. In a sense, government is accepted as a necessary evil. Without government, who would establish justice? Ensure domestic tranquility? Provide for the common defense? Promote the general welfare? Or secure the blessings of liberty to ourselves and our posterity? But a government powerful enough to serve these common interests also poses dangers. Such a government might exercise authority capriciously, intrude unnecessarily, choose improper means, or simply fail to do its job effectively. The problems of this profession thus have deep philosophical roots to which a school of government must be attentive.

The Kennedy School curriculum stresses analytic skills (in economics, statistics, and operations research); institutional sense (about organizations, politics, and feasibil-

Harvard President Derek Bok (JD '54).

ity); ethical sensitivity (appreciating the values affected by a problem and being able to analyze ethical dimensions of issues without falling victim to what I.A. Richards called "premature ultimates"); and a substantive orientation (including a willingness to wrap one's mind around the details of a policy problem whether it be income maintenance, budgeting, or defense strategy). The compleat public manager should be not only literate and numerate but also adept at pulling together diverse dimensions of an issue and taking responsibility, within the constitutional framework, to solve problems and produce public value.

Society has invested little in capturing lessons learned from successful public problem-solving. Its investment in learning about effective professional practice in business and medicine has been much greater. Harvard's Kennedy School, through its individual faculty members, its Institute of Politics, and its increasing number of research centers, endeavours to become the national center for *organized learning* about what effective public managers

know and do. The thousands of units of government constitute, in effect, workbenches and research labs. In city after city, mayors, city managers, and budget officers must cope with parallel problems from transportation to public safety to budgeting to community involvement. Some fail; some succeed. But what happens to the knowledge they gain? In some instances, they pass it on to their associates, but unfortunately, most of it stays in their own heads. As a society that offers new officials so little of the benefit of whatever their predecessors have learned, we pay dearly for repeated on-the-job training.

The Kennedy School aspires to become the missing half of this research laboratory: an organized, systematic effort to capture lessons learned. This requires an authentic curiosity both about policy problems and about what public managers actually do. Cases expose recurring management problems, identify successful and less successful practice in problem-solving, document better practice, and analyze and clarify it. Through case-study methodology, the School is becoming a

"Despite the difficulty of the issues our leaders face, despite the difficulty of managing our public institutions, we have not had a tradition of serious, careful preparation of positions of public leadership comparable to the preparation provided for those entering our great private professions. That is the *principal missing link* in American higher education today."
—*Harvard President Derek Bok ('54)*

The John F. Kennedy School of Government's "new" Littauer Center of Public Administration.

storehouse of knowledge about successful problem-solving.

The argument for a professional school of government is compelling. But was it not equally compelling in 1936, following the Great Depression and Franklin Roosevelt's first New Deal, when Lucius Littauer made a gift to Harvard to create an independent Faculty of Public Administration? Indeed, was it not even more compelling in 1960 when John F. Kennedy was elected president and embodied the hope for intelligence applied to new frontiers? Or in 1966 when the School was renamed in honor of President Kennedy, and President Johnson's Great Society was the order of the day?

John F. Kennedy once observed that "a rising tide lifts all boats." The corollary for a receding tide also holds. This being so, it could be argued that Harvard chose the worst of times to make a school of government its major initiative in graduate education. Recall the milestones. In 1969, as the Public Policy Program opened its doors, Richard Nixon entered the White House after a campaign against government. By

1973, when President Derek Bok's annual report focused on the School, the crimes of Watergate had reduced confidence in government to its lowest level in modern times. The election of Jimmy Carter in 1976 brought to Washington a president even more viscerally hostile to government than Nixon had been. In his 1981 inaugural address Ronald Reagan declared: "Government is not the solution to our problems. Government is the problem."

Harvard's prescience in choosing to be countercyclical is striking. Despite these objective factors, the School has made considerable progress over the past two decades in stretching toward Lucius Littauer's vision of 1936. Indeed as Harvard celebrates its 350th birthday and the School commemorates the 50th anniversary of its own founding, the John F. Kennedy School of Govern-

ment can surely stake its claim as a visible presence in the university, and increasingly on the national landscape.

Over the past decade, the School has emerged as Harvard's major new venture in graduate education in this era. Harvard's goal is to build a professional school that serves society's demand for excellence in government as its schools of Business, Law, and Medicine address analogous concerns in their respective private professions. It is attempting to create something that has never before existed.

Harvard's links with government, of course, go back to the University's earliest days. The College, the Law School, and other schools of the University have long sent their graduates into government and continue to do so. Since colonial times, Harvard graduates have accepted an obligation to promote excellence in

Lamont University Professor John T. Dunlop (AM '46 hon.) symbolizes the University's commitment to create a school of government with the highest standards of both academic and practical pursuits.

Below: Harvard's links with government go back to the University's earliest days. Eight signers of the Declaration of Independence—including Samuel Adams, John Hancock, and John Adams—were educated at Harvard. Shown here, the commemorative statue of John Harvard looks out over historic Harvard Yard.

"Government has never been much studied. . . . [It] will be studied. . . . The result in time will be improvements . . . in the condition of mankind."
—*John Adams ('55)*

President Franklin D. Roosevelt ('04), seated at left, addressed Harvard's Tercentenary in 1936.

government. Eight signers of the Declaration of Independence—including three prominent leaders of the American Revolution, Samuel Adams, John Hancock, and John Adams—were educated at Harvard. In this century, Harvard graduates have served as president of the United States for one year in every four. At Harvard's Tercentenary Celebration in 1936, President Franklin Roosevelt, class of 1904, proclaimed: "Harvard should train men to be citizens in that high Athenian sense which compels a man to live his life unceasingly aware that its civic significance is its most abiding." Harvard has accepted that challenge.

The University also designated the school of government, as the hub of the university-wide Program in Public Policy and Administration. Rather than seeking to duplicate the many competences relevant to government that already exist in Harvard's departments of Economics and Government and the schools of Law, Medicine, and Business, the School of Government mobilizes these resources to focus on central issues of public policy. By assembling in one professional school a critical mass of energy with a sustained concentration on public policy, the School of Government seeks to extend and enhance Harvard's contributions to public problem-solving.

If the School is the hub, one spoke connects Harvard with Washington. Of course, there are other such spokes. Henry Kissinger, James Schlesinger, Elliot Richardson, Zbigniew Brzezinski, Caspar Weinberger, and Donald Regan are only a few of the many national figures whose connection with the University began with the College or the Graduate School of Arts and Sciences or, as in the case of Daniel Patrick Moynihan, with appointment as a Harvard faculty professor. For such individuals, Harvard's commitment to this new venture engages their interests and provides in effect a second Harvard home. The School's own faculty, alumni, and associates are increasingly prominent in national affairs. Moynihan's Senate colleagues Larry Pressler and William Proxmire hold degrees from the School. Senators Jeff Bingaman, William Cohen, Don Riegle, Paul Sarbanes, and Paul Simon are former participants in executive programs or Fellows of the School's Institute of Politics. A much larger number of alumni and former associates serve in the House. Many members of the current House of Representatives have attended the Program for Newly Elected Members of Congress. And a legion of younger School alumni work for members of Congress, as, for example, Sheila Burke, recently appointed chief of staff to Senate majority leader Robert Dole.

From George Washington to

Jimmy Carter, administrations had no educational program to benefit new subcabinet appointees. In 1981, when the Reagan Administration decided to create such a program, it chose the John F. Kennedy School of Government at Harvard to develop the professional management component. Attorney General Edwin Meese (then counsel to the president), worked with Institute of Politics Director Jonathan Moore in developing Harvard's component. At an opening session of one of the first dozen programs, Meese commented:

Some Reaganites will find it odd that this administration has asked Harvard's Kennedy School to be our partner in this program. What you may find even more remarkable is that the Reagan Administration has the highest percentage of Harvard graduates among its cabinet and subcabinet appointees of any administration in American history—substantially exceeding the percentage in the administration of John F. Kennedy. But if you think this is strange, consider how it seems to me as a Yale man!

From the ranks of the School's faculty the Reagan Administration

Michael Dukakis departs for the State Capitol, taking with him Kennedy School staff and faculty: (front row from left to right) Associate Dean Ira Jackson became commissioner of revenue; Assistant to the Dean Susan Byers assisted in the Revenue Department; Building Manager Gregory Arnold worked for the superintendant of state offices; (back row from left to right) Director of the School's State and Local Executive Program Charles Kiereker became director of the Massachusetts Industrial Finance Agency; Governor-elect Michael Dukakis; Professor David Hamburg became president of the Carnegie Corporation; National Security Program Director Douglas Johnston left to start his own consulting firm; Lecturer Manuel Carballo became secretary of human services; and Director of the Forum Nicholas Mitropoulos became director of the Governor's Personnel Office.

Harvard President Derek Bok discusses international issues with a group of the School's Mason Fellows.

chose Richard Darman to become deputy chief of staff in the White House, Roger Porter as deputy director of the Domestic Policy Staff and counsel to the secretary of the treasury, and Chris DeMuth to direct the president's Regulatory Relief Program.

In Massachusetts the School has comparable links with the Democratic administration of Governor Michael Dukakis. Having served on the faculty from 1977 to 1980, Dukakis announced that his second gubernatorial term would be "a test of what I have learned and what we try to teach at the Kennedy School." His initial appointees to the cabinet included so many members of the School's faculty and administration (among them, Manny Carballo, Ira Jackson, and Nick Mitropoulos) that the dean had to negotiate with the governor a freeze on further hiring from the School's central ranks. Kennedy School graduates are found at all levels throughout the state government and in the State House. A special program for Massachusetts state officials has exposed some 300 of the state's top managers to the School's curriculum. Again to quote

Governor Dukakis: "The Kennedy School provides the talent, competence, and vision that this state and other states need to make government work."[2]

Cities around the country, and even the world, are also connected to the School. Mayors from Henry Cisneros in San Antonio and Xavier Suarez in Miami to Ronnie McClean in La Paz, Bolivia, come from the ranks of Master in Public Administration and Master in Public Policy graduates. A hundred others have attended the short Seminar on Mayoral Leadership and Transitions.

South of the border, in Mexico City, President Miguel de la Madrid (MPA 1965) assembled a cabinet that included Carlos Salinas de Gortari (MPA 1973, Ph.D. 1978) as minister of planning and budgets. Until Pierre Trudeau stepped down

as prime minister of Canada, graduates of the School were chief elected officers both north and south of U.S. borders. Halfway around the world in Singapore, Prime Minister Lee Kwan Yew is a former Fellow of the Institute of Politics, and a third of the members of his cabinet are graduates of Kennedy School degree programs. Indeed, many of the leaders of the anti-Marcos democratic experiment in the Philippines have close Harvard ties, including Evelio Javier (MPA, 1981), a former provincial governor of Antique, and a manager of Corazon Aquino's presidential campaign. Javier was murdered on February 11, 1986, apparently by supporters of President Marcos.

Among the School's approximately 700 students, some 400 are young men and women of the same high calibre as those in the Business

The Belfer Center for Public Management houses many of the School's research centers. Seen here from the gates of neighboring Eliot House.

School, Law School, and Medical School. They are enrolled in the School's two-year Master in Public Policy program, established in 1969. (Some are enrolled for both a Kennedy School degree and an M.B.A., J.D., or M.D.) Fifty or so others are Ph.D. candidates, hard to distinguish from those in Arts and Sciences except perhaps for their having some additional work experience. The remaining 250 are, however, very different from most other students in and around Harvard Yard. They have an average of ten years service in government. Many are from federal agencies or career services. Some have backgrounds on Capitol Hill. A large number are from state or local governments, including the fifty Mason Fellows who come from developing countries where they have served at subcabinet levels in key departments. For other students in the School and the University, these mid-career students are a rich resource for learning about the world of government and the world beyond the United States.

Even more distinctive are the 600 other "students" in the School's executive programs. These executive programs include Institute of Politics seminars for Newly Elected Members of Congress and Newly Elected Mayors; the White House seminars in Washington for new subcabinet appointees; two- to three-week programs for admirals, generals, and civilians of comparable standing from the national security arena, senior officials primarily from domestic agencies, and senior officials from state and local governments; an eight-week program for colonels and Navy captains and their civilian counterparts; and a thirteen-week program for new members of the federal Senior Executive Service. A constant flow of such highly experienced men and women challenges not only other students but the faculty. As one veteran faculty member advised a new faculty member about to teach in one of the executive programs, "Don't be nervous; just keep in mind that the group you are going to teach represents about a thousand years of experience."

If the first test of the School is the performance of its students in public service, the second test must be the School's contribution to the storehouse of knowledge about successful problem-solving. In addition to its Institute of Politics, where faculty, students, and practitioners join to study such subjects as presidential transition, campaign strategies, and the role of money in politics, the School has five major research centers and is about to add a sixth. The Center for Science and International Affairs sponsors work on such subjects as avoiding nuclear war and the ethics of nuclear strategy and publishes the journal *International Security*. The Energy and Environmental Policy Center has the unique distinction of being the only center in the country that focuses on both energy policy and environmental issues—including their interactions. The Center for

Health Policy and Management links the Kennedy School with the schools of Medicine and Public Health and Harvard-related hospitals. It includes an Institute for the Study of Smoking Behavior and Policy. The State, Local, and Intergovernmental Center, which includes the joint Harvard-M.I.T. Housing Center, is becoming a repository of knowledge about successful practice in local problem-solving. The Business and Government Center examines the changing roles of government and business in public problem-solving and connects research at the Kennedy and Business schools. A newly dedicated Joan Shorenstein Barone Center for the Press, Politics, and Public Policy will focus on interactions between the media and government.

To date these research centers and the School's faculty members have to their credit several hundred books, several thousand articles and cases, and countless presentations to legislative committees, executive commissions, learned societies, and lay audiences. The research output covers subjects from battlefield nuclear weapons to welfare and

Senator Edward M. Kennedy (AB '54)

New York Mayor Ed Koch

Cesar Chavez

America's public leaders face the Kennedy School audience in the Forum.

Thomas P. "Tip" O'Neill, Jr.

The Hon. Elliot Richardson (AB '41, LLB '44)

working mothers. Some of this research provides new tools with which to advance frontiers of analysis, including Howard Raiffa's work on decisions analysis, Frederick Mosteller's on exploratory data analysis, Mark Moore's on implementation analysis, and Richard Neustadt and Ernest May's on the uses of history in decisionmaking. Other research applies analysis to identify policy options for action on nuclear proliferation, energy vulnerability, poverty, American families, economic development, impacts of habits like smoking on health, and risks of nuclear war. In few, if any, places in the world, is comparable intellectual energy devoted to such a wide range of public policy issues.

The School's ARCO Public Affairs Forum has given Harvard, for the first time, a political union. It has been said that if one stands for long enough in Harvard Square, he will eventually see everyone he knows. If one just sits in the Forum, he will encounter most of the major actors in contemporary American politics and policymaking. Literally and figuratively the center of the School's main building, the Forum

ABC newsman Ted Koppel using the Forum and a Kennedy School student audience for a special production of "Nightline."

A debate in the Forum among the 1984 presidential primary contenders: Senator Alan Cranston, Reverend Jesse Jackson, former Senator George McGovern, Senator Gary Hart, Senator John Glenn, former Vice President Walter Mondale, and Senator Ernest Hollings.

New York Congressman Jack Kemp pushes on the supply side.

Reagan foreign policy witness Jeanne Kirkpatrick is cross-examined.

Senator Christopher Dodd discusses arms control negotiations and his opposition to aiding the *contras* in Central America.

A segment of the "Advocates" is filmed in the Forum two nights before the 1984 presidential election. Moderator Governor Michael Dukakis makes the Mondale case.

is a five-story atrium ringed by small seating areas. In the daytime it encourages informal conversation among students and faculty. At night it becomes Harvard's town meeting hall programmed by the Institute of Politics. From debates among presidential candidates or gubernatorial aspirants to policy arguments by cabinet officers and foreign leaders, Forum events allow the Harvard community to see and hear the people who shape policy. The late Olaf Palme gave there the Jerry Wurf Memorial Lecture on "Employment and Welfare." During the 1984 campaign the "Advocates" televised from the Forum a debate pitting Jack Kemp and Jeanne Kirkpatrick against Mondale backers Mike Dukakis and Christopher Dodd. Often likened to the Oxford Union, the Forum has become the University's arena for debate.

These faculty and students, research and special programs all strive toward a common objective. They recognize that the problems government addresses are fundamental problems from avoiding nuclear war to building more liveable cities, from assuring the competitiveness of the American economy to promoting international economic development. None of these problems will simply solve themselves. None can be solved by government acting alone. The special challenge of public service is to shape frameworks that encourage effective working relations among the holders of power —both public and private. Whether the issue is promoting employment, building international financial institutions, or ensuring stable economic growth, public problem-solvers must engage the energies of leaders from all sectors of society in the search for solutions. The Kennedy School stands at the frontier of their effort.

Consistent with the School's spirit of inquiry, former Dean Don Price suggested that the happy coincidence of the University's and the School's anniversaries provided occasion for preparing a case study of the School's own development. This book is not, of course, a full history of the School. That would have to document the careers of the thousands who have been students at the School or exposed to its programs. A full history would also have to tell what went on in the School's classrooms and myriad research projects. This book merely recounts some of what was thought and done by successive presidents of the University, deans, and members of the faculty as they made the decisions that shaped the School.

During this milestone year, the John F. Kennedy School of Government looks back at conditions fifty years ago and forward to possibilities fifty years hence. This review is a source of pride and of hope but also of humility. The School has come far, thanks to all those who have invested here their scarcest resources: themselves. The foundation they have laid gives us inspiration and confidence as we recognize how much farther the School has yet to go.

—Dean Graham T. Allison, Jr.

1

Origins

What is today the John Fitzgerald Kennedy School of Government traces its origin to the Graduate School of Public Administration, established in 1936. A year earlier, Lucius Nathan Littauer (Harvard class of 1878), a retired New York glove manufacturer, former member of Congress, and prominent philanthropist, gave Harvard $2 million to found an independent school of public administration. The School created by Littauer's endowment was in many ways very different from the one that exists today. But there are also striking similarities that bespeak fifty years of continuity. Throughout its history the School's underlying purpose has remained constant—to strive for the highest possible level of professional training in keeping with Harvard's commitment to exacting standards of academic excellence and intellectual achievement.

Such a tradition did not, of course, spring into existence overnight. In fact, when Lucius Littauer came forward with the offer to endow a new school, it was far from clear, from Harvard's experience or from that of other universities, just what the professional study of government and public administration ought to include and what it could or should hope to accomplish. Though the number of institutions offering such programs had risen steadily since the turn of the century to around 100 by the 1930s, the quality and content of curriculums varied considerably. Some focused on pre-entry training, others on post-entry training. In large metropolitan areas the programs were often part-time or given in night school for the benefit of those already employed in government agencies. Most programs were technical or specialized. Few emphasized the general capacity for and understanding of problem-solving.

The dozen best-known and most successful schools stressed education in the social sciences, though usually with some eye to practical applications. The University of Southern California's School of Government (the largest of its kind in the country) emphasized *scientific management*, a concept already

Lucius N. Littauer (AB '78), Harvard's first football coach, a glove manufacturer, and a congressman from New York, gave in 1936 the largest single donation Harvard had ever received as a gift to establish Harvard's Graduate School of Public Administration.

"The constant need in the progress of government administration which this new School must meet is for clearer, more lucid thinking through better-trained men—men who must in the future with certainty and integrity solve the economic and administrative problems of their day."
—*Lucius N. Littauer ('78)*

well known in the private sector, which was popularized in the 1920s by the School's founder and first dean Emery E. Olson, as applicable also in government. Olson believed that the teaching of sound management techniques would improve the quality and effectiveness of public administration. Syracuse University's Maxwell School concentrated on teaching management skills in such technical fields as health, welfare, and public works. New York University provided more narrow inservice training, though it also offered independent field work for students who lacked work experience.

The idea of Harvard's training public servants dates from the turn of the century. In 1899, following the war with Spain that brought America an overseas colonial empire, Archibald Cary Coolidge, a professor of history in Harvard's Faculty of Arts and Sciences, proposed to President Charles William Eliot the creation of "a training School for diplomacy and the government service, a little like the Ecole des Sciences Politiques in Paris." Coolidge suggested a special department in the division of

history and economics, "with some change in title and arrangement."[3]

Eliot was receptive and appointed a committee to investigate the idea. Coolidge meanwhile tried to interest A. Lawrence Lowell, the distinguished Boston attorney who later succeeded Eliot as president of Harvard. He failed. Lowell saw no merit in the project. Instead, Lowell endorsed the creation of a school to provide training for business management. Thus the result of Coolidge's initiative was the Harvard Business School, which opened in 1908.

As the University's president from 1909 to 1933, Lowell continued to oppose Harvard's offering special training for government service. He questioned whether there was sufficient demand. More than that, he rejected the premise that government service resembled professions like law or medicine or even business. Lowell approved of government by amateurs.

At the groundbreaking for the Littauer Center in 1937: Graduate School of Public Administration Dean John H. Williams (AM '16, Ph.D. '19), Harvard President James B. Conant (AB '14, Ph.D. '16), and Lucius N. Littauer (AB '78).

The Littauer Endowment

By the time Lowell stepped down in 1933, the Great Depression had led to an expanded government at the local and state as well as federal levels. James Bryant Conant, Lowell's successor, harbored no prejudice against the University's offering professional training for public service. With the value of many of Harvard's investments dwindling and donations to the University falling off, it was a propitious time for Lucius Littauer to offer to endow a new school of public administration.

Conant did not leap to accept the Littauer gift. A scientist by training, whose central concern as Harvard's president was to protect the quality of its intellectual environment, Conant believed that the University should proceed slowly and weigh carefully each and every move it made in carrying out the donor's wishes.

In fact, as Conant pointed out in his memoirs, Harvard already had, or was in the process of organizing, several public administration programs. These included a program on

public business, announced by the Business School in December 1934, and the appointment the following spring of a Committee on Preparation for the Government Service, headed by Professor Carl Joachim Friedrich of the Government Department, to advise recent college graduates on further training they might need to enter the civil service. In addition, the Economics Department, the Law School, the Engineering faculty, the School of City Planning, and the School of Public Health all considered themselves uniquely qualified to give specialized instruction in various aspects of public administration. Obviously, there was no lack of interest or enthusiasm within the Harvard faculty. What was most

sorely needed, Conant believed, was an effective coordinating mechanism to arrest the growing competition, not necessarily a new school to duplicate instruction already being offered. "When Mr. Littauer made his offer of a generous gift," Conant recalled, "he threw a golden apple into a Harvard family already in disagreement."[4]

Since Lucius Littauer left no personal papers that might reveal his motivations, it is hard to pinpoint how and why he decided to endow a school of public administration. According to his close friend and personal secretary Harry Starr, Littauer's immediate reason was to dispose of income that had built up from his late wife's estate. A septuagenarian with no immediate heirs,

President Derek Bok (JD '54, AB '71) presents Harry Starr (AB '21, LLB '24), president of the Littauer Foundation, a bound volume of the School's programs and progress at a dinner commemorating the fortieth anniversary of the Littauer endowment for the establishment of the Graduate School of Public Administration.

Littauer saw no point in keeping the money. "Unless there is some way in which we can use these funds for the public benefit," he told Starr, "I don't really want them."[5] Knowing Littauer well, Starr suggested that he consider endowing a school of government or public service.

Politics and government had occupied much of Littauer's life. A close personal friend of Theodore Roosevelt since their days together at Harvard College, Littauer identified with the progressive wing of the Republican party. When then Governor Roosevelt came out in support of civil service reform, Littauer's lobbying efforts smoothed the legislation's passage through the state assembly. As a member of the

U.S. House of Representatives from 1897 to 1907, Littauer often served as Roosevelt's agent or floor manager as, for example, in the hard fight of 1903 to create a Department of Commerce and Labor. Observers, including crusty House Speaker "Uncle Joe" Cannon, agreed that Littauer was the de facto House leader and would have become its formal leader had he not chosen to retire from politics in order to devote more time to business and philanthropy. Starr's suggestion thus had immediate appeal for Littauer.

Another person who apparently gave advice similar to Starr's was Littauer's confidant and occasional legal adviser Felix Frankfurter, then a member of the Harvard Law

School faculty. Though Frankfurter, a liberal academician, and Littauer, a conservative businessman, may have viewed politics from opposite perspectives, they agreed that the Depression and the New Deal had transformed the role of government in the affairs of the country. They also agreed that this created a need for çivil servants of the highest possible calibre and training. Establishing a professional school seemed the logical first step toward accomplishing these objectives.

Littauer thought naturally of Harvard. He had graduated in the class of 1878, been a member of the varsity crew, and been the first coach of the football team. He felt a lifelong affection for Harvard and made the university many gifts, among them the Nathan Littauer Professorship of Jewish Literature and Philosophy in memory of his father and the donation to the Harvard College Library of his personal collection of nearly 15,000 volumes of Hebrew literature. Littauer believed that no other institution in the country was more fit than Harvard to house the school he envisioned.

Drawing up the terms for Lit-

> "We had the vision that it was possible . . . to devise a school which might, in time, attain the intellectual prestige and acceptance of Harvard's other professional schools."
>
> —*Harry Starr ('21)*

tauer's $2 million gift fell jointly to Starr and Wallace B. Donham, dean of the Harvard Business School. Starr suggested that the School be named Littauer, citing the Lawrence Scientific School as a precedent. Donham said the example no longer held since the Lawrence name had already been removed. Moreover, it was his understanding that Harvard would never again name a school for an individual. Donham offered to name in Littauer's honor the building that would house the School. Satisfied that this was a fair offer, Starr dropped the matter.[6] Many years later, Harvard decided to make an exception to its policy and named the School of Government after John F. Kennedy.

The letter of gift, dated November 13, 1935, settled the issue of the School's name simply by calling it the Graduate School of Public Administration. The stated purpose was to provide training "in a broad way for public service." Littauer's donation was to be not less than $2 million. At the time it was the largest single gift from an individual donor Harvard had ever received. One quarter of the money was to be used for construction of the Littauer Center of Public Administration; the balance would go in escrow as an endowment fund. (Later, when he learned that the construction fund was too small to erect a building on the location he wanted, Littauer donated an additional $250,000.) With the letter, the University took the first formal step toward establishing what would eventually become the John F. Kennedy School of Government.

This was, of course, not the University's first step toward training men and women for public service. That it had done continually since its founding in 1636. One of its first graduates (class of 1643) was George (later Sir George) Downing, who had a notorious career as a diplomat and politician serving King Charles II. (Downing Street, where British prime ministers work and live, is named after him.) Later graduates included eight of the signers of the Declaration of Independence and many magistrates, members of legislatures, governors, members of Congress, cabinet officers, and presidents. The acceptance of the Littauer gift marked a new departure

Founding fathers at the dedication of the Littauer Center in May 1939: Dean John H. Williams (AM '16, Ph.D. '19), former Harvard President A. Lawrence Lowell (AB '77), Leverett Saltonstall (AB '14, LLB '17, LLD '42), Lucius N. Littauer (AB '78), Harvard President James B. Conant (AB '14, Ph.D. '16), and Charles F. Adams (LLB '15).

only in singling out public service as a career for which the University could provide specialized training. What remained uncertain for many years thereafter was whether the University would treat this career as a profession like law or business.

The Dodds Report

After Littauer's gift had been offered and accepted, much remained to be done. The new building had to be constructed. More important, weighty issues regarding the School's administration, faculty, and program needed to be resolved.

The most difficult problem had to do with the School's purpose. Littauer had sketched his hopes with some precision. First, he had asked

that there be "a separate School," organized "as a separate and well-knit educational unit" and composed of a "new faculty" with its own dean and "three full-time professors, assistant professors or instructors." If the University saw fit, it could make appointments "drawn from the correlated schools and departments . . . to serve part time on the faculty of the School." The curriculum should be "directed to a professional objective and the development of training in government as a profession, and not simply to education in government as a branch of learning." As a general guide, Littauer suggested that instruction include "history, politics and economics of the past." Finally, he asked that the School offer at least two years' training, leading to the awarding of some form of degree.[7]

Though existing departments and

schools at Harvard applauded Littauer's gift, they were none too keen on acquiring a new rival. Some, like the Business School and the Government Department, already had programs in public administration and sought to make themselves the beneficiaries. Others staked claims of their own. No one stepped forward to champion the wholly new undertaking described by Littauer.

In hope of finding some consensus or at least postponing his own moment of choice, Conant appointed a six-member planning commission chaired by President Harold W. Dodds of Princeton University. The other commission members were Leonard D. White, professor of political science at the University of Chicago and member of the U.S. Civil Service Commission; William B. Munro, professor of history and government at the California Institute of Technology, formerly at Harvard; and three members of the Harvard faculty—Dean Wallace B. Donham of the Business School, Professor Harold H. Burbank of the Economics Department, and Professor Morris B. Lambie of the Government Department.

The School's first dean, John H. Williams (AM '16, Ph.D. '19).

Conant's concern was apparent in the charter he gave Dodds. While Littauer's gift had been generous, it was not large enough to endow new professorships in any significant number. This fact, combined with awareness of claims likely to be made by existing schools and departments, led Conant to write Dodds that "a large majority of the faculty members of the new School will be members of the present faculties of the University and will thus hold a dual position, and that most of the courses of instruction will properly be those already given in the different faculties." Conant characterized the prospective school as primarily "a center for bringing together the diverse activities in our different faculties which are already concerned one way or another with training men for the government service."[8]

On December 1, 1936, following nearly a year of study, the Dodds Commission rendered its report. In general, the report followed Conant's guidance. It urged extreme care in planning and organizing the School. It conceded that initially the existing departments and other gradu-

ate schools of the University should provide the bulk of the faculty and course offerings.

Over the longer term, the Dodds Commission urged that every effort be made to give the School a distinctive character. The Commission report suggested new courses tailored to professional instruction in such areas as public policy, economic and political statistics and analysis, public administration, business phases of public policy, and practical politics; a mixed student body of those interested in or already pursuing careers in government; and an organization—as Littauer had earlier suggested—consisting of a dean, a separate budget, and a separate faculty to include three or four instructors "whose association is primarily with the new institution." The report also called for basic research to create an "atmosphere of intellectual earnestness."[9]

To get from the near term to the longer term, the Dodds Commission recommended a year or more of additional exploratory study involving consultations in Cambridge between experienced public officials and Harvard faculty members to develop the

curriculum in more detail. Conant promptly endorsed this suggestion and with the aid of a grant of $65,000 from the Rockefeller Foundation began planning a series of conferences to be held in the spring of 1937. Meanwhile, on December 7, 1936, the Harvard Corporation made its first twelve Graduate School of Public Administration (GSPA) faculty appointments (all of whom already held appointments elsewhere in the University), thus signaling the School's official beginning. As dean, Conant later named Professor John H. Williams of the Economics Department.

Further Deliberations

Beginning in 1937 Conant met regularly with the newly appointed

Alvin H. Hansen (AM '42 hon.), one of the first faculty members of the School, from 1936 to 1956.

members of the GSPA faculty to discuss the School's future and to arrange for the upcoming series of conferences involving some seventy-five local, state, and federal officials as consultants. Early on in these deliberations, Conant made it plain that he considered the School's first five years or so to be experimental. Money—or rather the lack of it—was in most instances the decisive factor. Conant insisted that the only practical course of action was for the School to utilize the University's existing resources to the maximum extent before setting out to develop its own. He reiterated his opinion that the School should operate in a coordinating capacity. Describing it as a "switching station," he saw it drawing on existing faculty and courses to provide students with diversified professional training.

The findings of the consultants reinforced Conant's position. There could be no course of instruction useful to public administrators, they reported, that was not now offered, or could not readily be offered, by existing branches of the University. It followed that rather than attempt-

ing to devise new and independent courses of instruction, the School should concentrate on bringing existing courses to the attention of its students. These students should be career public officials with at least several years of on-the-job experience. For the time being, the consultants saw no need to award a degree. Should the School choose to embark on new activities, they advised, it should eschew the vocational or management-type training offered at most other institutions and instead offer seminars dealing with public policy problems in their broadest sense.

The Graduate School of Public Administration, which welcomed its first students in 1937, was not yet the separate professional school that Littauer had envisioned. Given the circumstances of the time, however, Conant's cautious approach was sensible, perhaps inevitable. Littauer himself was not disappointed. Conant consulted him about the proposed appointment of Alvin Harvey Hansen, then a member of the faculty of the University of Minnesota, to a joint professorship in the Graduate School of Public Ad-

ministration and the Department of Economics. Similar joint arrangements, Conant explained, would apply to all other faculty members. In reply to this proposal, Littauer said: "I am in entire accord with the arrangements outlined . . . regarding the appointment of Professor Hansen or any similar appointment and am entirely willing that the phrase 'full-time' in my letter of gift should be so interpreted in this and in any subsequent appointments of new men to the faculty of the school."[10]

The eminent M.I.T. economist, Paul Samuelson, wrote in March 1986, "Only after the Littauer School of Public Administration—that is what we called it—was established can we date the Harvard renaissance in macroeconomics." At the time of Hansen's appointment, Harvard's leading economists were all of the neoclassical school, among them Joseph Schumpeter, Wassily Leontief, Edward Chamberlin, and O.H. Taylor. Samuelson, a neo-Keynesian, comments that their joint volume (with others), *The Economics of the Recovery Program*, published in 1934, "documents for the record the sad irrelevance of neoclassical economics for the great depression."[11] Observing that Keynes "should obviously have been invited to the tercentenary assemblage of the world's greatest scholars [but] political bias black-balled his selection," Samuelson ascribes the appointment of Hansen to "miscalculation." Hansen brought Keynesian economics to Harvard. "He turned out to be better than his electors wanted, and an Elizabethan Age ensued at Harvard." Samuelson continues:

John Williams, the first Dean of the Littauer School, formed with Alvin Hansen a remarkable duo. If to teach is to affirm, then Williams should have become a banker full time. But if to teach is to raise doubt, Williams was a brilliant success. Actually, Williams' cracker-barrel, seemingly relaxed, manner made him a splendid teacher. He recruited hundreds of undergraduates to major in economics.

Inevitably Hansen, the pioneer of a new scientific paradigm, stole the show and attracted the bulk of graduate students destined to become eminent. . . . It does both Hansen and Williams enormous credit that they never undercut each other in the classroom or outside. It was rarely like this in the continental universities and certainly not in the LSE, Cambridge, and Chicago bullpens, where the disciples of the competing stars were pitted against each other not merely on class and ideological issues but also on mundane questions of methodology. . . . Since Hansen had the disproportionate power for aggression, I suppose he merits the greater praise. Still, it would have been understandable if Williams had nursed resentment that his turf had been taken over. And yet that private individual could say, on the occasion of both men's retirement, that Alvin Hansen had been the best friend he had ever had in academic life.[12]

Reflecting the faculty's acceptance of the consultants' suggestion, Dean Williams' letter to Conant about the Hansen appointment highlights the most original feature of the new Harvard School—the emphasis on seminar research in substantive public policy areas that was to become its trademark. With periodic variations in focus from domestic to foreign affairs, from economic issues to political issues, this emphasis on policy, as opposed to public administration alone, has persisted through the subsequent fifty years. If Conant and his advisers had hurried to carry out Littauer's wishes, or if Littauer had been less patient and understanding, the Kennedy School of the 1980s might have had a longer history as an independent institution, but it might also be very different in character.

When Littauer gave the additional $250,000 for construction, he knew that the money was to provide a building large enough to serve as a social sciences center, housing the Economics and Government departments, not to house a separate faculty. From time to time he expressed fear that these two large and well-entrenched departments might so dominate the School that it would be unable to develop its own identity. "The answer I always made to him," Dean Williams recalled, "was that we hoped and believed that the School would be an agency for focusing the interests of the departments, at the graduate level, on problems of public policy and administration; and it was on this understanding that Mr. Littauer consented to our changing his original plan for a separate school."[13]

2

The First Two Decades

Between the 1930s and the 1950s the development of the Graduate School of Public Administration followed the general lines determined in the earlier exploratory phase. It remained essentially an adjunct of previously existing departments. It nevertheless acquired a distinctive student body. Its public policy seminars and other research activities increasingly focused on issues different from those central to the academic disciplines of economics and political science. These trends underscored the question of whether the School's adjunct status could or should be continued.

"Littauer"

"Littauer" first acquired identity as a building. Hunt Hall in Harvard Yard served its faculty as temporary quarters. In August 1936, at President Conant's invitation, Lucius Littauer came to Cambridge during an oppressive heatwave to survey a number of possible locations for a perma-

nent home. He found two especially promising—one near the corner of Mt. Auburn and Holyoke Streets and the other on Kirkland Street, overlooking Harvard Square, between the Yard and the Law School. The old Hemenway Gymnasium had stood there. Eventually, he and Conant decided to put the School on the latter site.

The new Littauer Center, begun in May 1938 and dedicated a year later, reflected the donor's high aspirations.A four-story structure built of New England granite in a Georgian design, it was nearly twice as large as originally planned thanks to Littauer's additional donation of $250,000. It had an auditorium and lounge, eight large seminar rooms, a central reading room, cubicles for graduate students, and a library with a 250,000-volume capacity. That both the Economics and Government departments were to have their offices in the building gave them a dominant presence in the School from the beginning.

Littauer Center circa 1949.

The old Hemenway Gym, torn down in order to build the Littauer Center in 1937.

Students

The original GSPA faculty established a highly selective enrollment policy. "By stressing quality to the exclusion of quantity," Dean Williams explained at the dedication ceremonies for the first Littauer Center, "we hope to give the new School somewhat the character of a super-graduate school."[14] The School initially admitted only a few Littauer Fellows. Not "students" in the normally accepted sense, these were public officials on leave of absence for a year of inservice study in Cambridge. The desired candidate for a Littauer fellowship was a man no older than thirty-five, with three to ten years of experience and an assured position in public service.

Almost all students received financial support. In most cases this was a stipend of $1,500 to cover living expenses and tuition (in 1986 dollars this would amount to about $7,500 after tuition). Students were awarded a certificate of attendance at the end of the year.

Part of the rationale for enrolling only Littauer Fellows was an argu-

Hunt Hall, former home of the Fogg Art Museum and offices of Dean Williams from 1937 to 1939.

The first Littauer Center opened in 1939.

ment that the School made the most effective use of its resources by concentrating on men already established in public service careers. Not all members of the faculty agreed with this argument, however, and it became a subject of frequent debate at early faculty meetings. The principal objection was that inservice Fellows failed to meet the test of high quality, at least intellectually. This was reported to have been the experience of the School of Public Health. An additional argument against the Fellows program was its high per-student cost. This debate eventually engendered a decision to accept a wider range of students.

In 1939 the School began to admit Administration Fellows, young men usually fresh out of college. The type was not new to Harvard. The Committee on Preparation for the Government Service, headed by Professor C.J. Friedrich, had for some years been recruiting such students. Friedrich simply transferred the program to the Graduate School of Public Administration. Then, in the spring of 1940, because of the expansion of governmental activity and the growing demand for better

training of civil servants, the faculty agreed to branch out further by admitting each year approximately a dozen tuition students whose selection would be subject to the same academic standards as fellowship holders.

Coinciding with the enlargement of the student body and the School's increasingly active role within the University came a decision to establish degree programs. Littauer and Administration Fellows were already eligible to seek degrees in the Graduate School of Arts and Sciences if they chose to do so. Students who would pay tuition, it was thought, should be entitled to degrees. With consent from Conant and the governing boards, the GSPA faculty created the Master in Public Administration (MPA), attainable upon completion of one year of satisfactory work by students with significant experience and after two years by students with little or none, and a Doctor of Public Administration (Dr. P.A.), with requirements initially similar to those for a Ph.D. in economics or government. In addition, the Economics and Government departments established a

joint degree, a Ph.D. in Political Economy and Government, intended mainly for students enrolled in the GSPA.

These decisions were made against the backdrop of events leading to World War II. For a brief time after Pearl Harbor, the School maintained business as usual. By the beginning of the 1942 autumn term, however, it could no longer do so. The number of qualified applicants for scholarships plummeted. Many faculty members went into uniform or joined OSS or went to work in a wartime Washington agency. The School and University were unable to offer the usual range of courses to those students who did come.

The faculty remaining in Cambridge considered closing down for the duration. Other parts of the University, such as the Business School, found that the severe shortage of recent college graduates left no choice but to suspend regular instruction for the duration of the war. The GSPA's Visiting Committee recommended that the School not follow this example. The Committee took the view that the newness of the School and its experi-

mental character underscored the importance of preserving continuity.[15] The faculty accepted that position. It even managed to maintain the student body at about its prewar size—around thirty-five students a year—but with a different mix of students. Unlike before the war, now fully half came from foreign countries, chiefly Latin America and Canada. Some came as Littauer or Administration Fellows, but most were admitted on a tuition basis under arrangements such as those Harvard established with the Central Bank of Argentina, which sent two new students each year to study economics.

Another difference, of greater long-term significance, was that some of the students were women. The faculty voted early in 1943 to open fellowships to "a limited number of women with administrative experience."[16] Several members of the Board of Overseers expressed apprehension lest the admission of women prove to be "another step toward co-education,"[17] apparently overlooking the fact that students at Radcliffe had been eligible to take courses in the School since 1939.

"Littauer thought naturally of Harvard. He had graduated in the class of 1878, been a member of the varsity crew, and been the first coach of the football team. He felt a lifelong affection for Harvard and made the university many gifts. . . . Littauer believed that no other institution in the country was more fit than Harvard to house the school he envisioned."

But it was to be 1956 before the faculty voted to admit women to the School on an unrestricted basis, ending the requirement that they first had to qualify for a fellowship.

After the war, returning veterans surged into colleges and graduate schools. Harvard tried to limit admissions under a quota formula, but the formula worked better in some parts of the University than in others. Having struggled to fill its classrooms during the war, the Littauer Center now found itself brimming with an overabundance of eager students. Most were returning servicemen with little or no other career experience. In 1946–47 the school registered sixty-three students. In the fall of 1947 the figure jumped to seventy-seven. Over the next few years enrollment climbed more slowly, eventually reaching a high of around 100 students in the early 1950s. Thereafter it dropped, as did applications for admission. By the middle of the decade it stabilized at around eighty-five, which most faculty members then accepted as the School's ideal size.

For quite a while it was hard to tell which of these students really

belonged to the School. During the decade immediately following the war, only about half the students enrolled as candidates solely for the degree of Master in Public Administration (MPA). Many others registered also as candidates for doctoral degrees in Arts and Sciences. By the mid-1950s the confusion lessened. Almost all applicants were by now coming to the school only as MPA candidates. The vast majority were older and more mature students with government backgrounds. Many were on leave of absence from their jobs. Younger students, it seemed, had lost interest in public service during the era of Joe McCarthy and *The Man in the Grey Flannel Suit*.

All the while, a sizable number of foreign students enrolled in the School. They made up annually between one-fifth and one-quarter of the School's population. Most of these students came from Canada, Latin America, and Western Europe, although a growing number were from Asia. Briefly during the late 1940s and early 1950s the School also sponsored a special program for German students. They were never

officially enrolled but came to Cambridge for a semester at a time to become more familiar with the functioning of democratic institutions. The program died because of immigration restrictions.

While some faculty members applauded the late 1950s' return to normalcy, others complained that the academic background of many applicants left something to be desired. This led the School in some cases to set aside standard admissions requirements. There was also increased pressure to provide financial aid. Although the Foreign Service, the armed services, and a few other federal agencies had funds to subsidize advanced training for their employees, most did not. (This condition was not remedied until 1958 when Congress passed the Government Employees' Training Act with

Senator Joseph S. Clark, then chairman of the GSPA Visiting Committee, playing a decisive role.) Few state and local governments had any such funds. Since government officials, particularly those with families, were apt to require financial assistance to pursue their education, the size of fellowship grants became a serious strain on the School's budget.

As the proportion of foreign students from less-developed countries rose, so, too, did the need for financial support. The School developed during its first two decades a large and distinctive student body. Many of its alumni had risen to high station in local, state, or federal bureaucracies and in governments abroad. Many faculty members, however, found it less appealing to teach these students than to teach more traditional students in Arts and Sciences, and the University was fast approaching the point where it would have to decide whether the GSPA student body was affordable.

Programs

The development of a distinctive GSPA curriculum did not keep pace with the development of a distinctive student body. The School's first catalog announced that it would offer "special group seminars, conducted on a research basis, in which questions of broad governmental policy may be studied." These seminars were taught by members of the GSPA faculty whose principal appointments were in other faculties. They were listed as offerings of the departments of Economics and Government for students in the Graduate School of Arts and Sciences and then simply cross listed as GSPA courses. These courses enrolled many Ph.D. candidates who were not in the GSPA. Even so, they quickly acquired a character somewhat different from standard graduate courses in the two departments.

The first volume of *Public Policy,* the School's yearbook, appeared in 1940. Each volume usually had one or more central themes taken from one of the School's seminars. Illustrative of the practice (and the times)

was the 1941 issue devoted in part to budgetary and fiscal problems and in part to defense issues. It provided students and faculty alike with an outlet for publishing the results of their research. Publication was discontinued during World War II but resumed in 1953 under the joint editorship of professors C.J. Friedrich and John Kenneth Galbraith.

In Conant's view the faculty's adoption of this statement (subsequently approved by the Harvard Corporation on June 19) did much to solidify the School's future and its relationship to the rest of the University. Almost any alternative policy would have caused him problems. Having accepted Littauer's gift, the University was obligated to maintain some program of public service education. On the other hand, any program more ambitious

than that endorsed by the faculty would require new money. With an annual endowment income of less than $60,000, the School was already hard put to fund fellowships and research grants, build its library, and contribute to faculty salaries. Financially, the most comfortable arrangement was for the School to be supplemental to the Economics and Government departments.

In accordance with the postwar plan, two new seminars in public policy were inaugurated. Although they were also given as joint offerings in the Economics and Government departments, they were without question courses designed principally for the GSPA. Their content had been carefully planned during the war, with the clear intention that they would provide a unifying course of instruction that all students enrolled in the School would be expected to take.

Conant had scheduled a reassessment of the School's activities at the end of its first five years, although the war forced postponement. In March 1944 he urged the faculty to think seriously of what they wanted the School to become. Though this

Professor Arthur Smithies (Ph.D. '35) taught political economy in the School from 1950 to 1978.

was two and one half months before the Normandy landings, and both the European and Pacific wars teetered in uncertain balance, Conant was already looking toward the war's end and an inevitable influx of returning veterans. "We are now in a transition period," he observed, "during which clear-cut offerings should be developed in the various fields of University activities."[18]

In response the GSPA faculty on May 23, 1944, endorsed a statement of policy affirming as a matter of principle the School's adjunct status. The statement was drafted by Dean Williams. Though it urged cooperation with other faculties, especially that of the Business School, the statement endorsed the School's central dependence on the Economics and Government departments. In outlining a postwar program, the statement called for two new courses—one in economic analysis and public policy and another in governmental administration and public policy. But it specifically rejected the idea that these or other courses offered by the School should be the basis for a separate and distinct curriculum.[19]

The economics seminar covered such subjects as taxation and budget. It was designed to introduce noneconomists to methods of economic analysis and to apply those methods to live public policy issues. It was taught by Edward S. Mason and Professor Arthur Smithies, an Australian-born expert on U.S. budgetary processes. The government seminar offered a similar introduction to political science. It was taught by professors John Gaus and Merle Fainsod, the latter a specialist in American government who by the 1950s had become the leading U.S. authority on Soviet government. The seminar drew heavily on contemporary examples. It contributed to the creation of the Inter-University Case Program, initially centered at the University of Syracuse.

Research

The School was originally conceived as a center for research as well as teaching. In early budgets, half to two-thirds of the income from endowment was set aside to bring consultants or visiting scholars to Cambridge and provide research support for the School's seminars. Some of this money paid for secretarial and telephone services for professors in the departments of Economics and Government who conducted the seminars, since the Faculty of Arts and Sciences did not at the time underwrite such luxuries. With postwar inflation, these charges came to absorb most of the School's otherwise uncommitted income. Not until the 1960s, when the Faculty of Arts and Sciences assumed responsibility for office services, did this budgetary strain ease.

Faculty members meanwhile sought and obtained outside financial support for their research. Thus over the years a number of special research and training projects were conducted, often centering on one of the seminars and involving special

Arthur A. Maass (MPA '41, Ph.D. '49), professor of government in the School from 1951 to 1984.

financing for fellowships and research staff. Two of the oldest and best known were a seminar on labor economics and collective bargaining taught by professors Sumner H. Slichter and John T. Dunlop and a seminar on agriculture, forestry, and land use taught by Professor John D. Black.

During the 1950s the list of such seminars and programs lengthened. The Ford Foundation underwrote a Defense Studies program; the Rockefeller Foundation, a Water Resources Development program; and the Rockefeller Brothers Fund together with the Ford Foundation, a New York Metropolitan Region Study.

Out of these programs came many monographs, including *Industrial Relations Systems* by Dunlop; Samuel P. Huntington's seminal analysis of differences between quantitative

and qualitative arms races, published in the 1958 issue of *Public Policy*; Arthur Maass' *Muddy Waters: The Army Engineers and the Nation's Rivers*; and Raymond Vernon's *Anatomy of a Metropolis*. These works and others were recognized as important contributions in the disciplines of economics and political science, but they also had an extra element. They were informed by the authors' interaction with people who had immediate problems to solve. They were contributions not only to theory but to the solution of real-world, practical problems.

Bordering on the frontier between the realms of theory and action was the School's program to assist the governments of Pakistan and Iran. In the early 1950s these two governments launched large-scale modernization drives. Professor Edward S. Mason had succeeded Williams as GSPA dean in 1948. Mason had taken a Ph.D. in economics at Harvard in the 1920s, pausing on the way for a B.Litt. from Oxford. As a member of the Harvard Economics Department, he consulted for the Labor Department during the 1930s

and during World War II took leave to head up economics research for the OSS. After the war he held posts in the State Department and the World Bank and was chief adviser to the American delegation at the Moscow Foreign Ministers Conference of 1947. At the urging of the Ford Foundation, Mason agreed to organize an advisory group to assist Pakistan, and later another group to help Iran, with development planning. Through the GSPA Mason recruited advisers to work in Cambridge and abroad and to provide such studies and reports as the governments involved might require.

The project in Pakistan led to the creation of a new group of students —Public Service Fellows in Economic Development. "It was clear," Mason recalled, "that there were not very many trained economists in Pakistan . . . It was this realization that further training would be highly desirable, not only for Pakistanis but for others, that led me to set up the Public Service Fellows Program in Harvard's School of Public Administration."[20] The Ford Foundation provided money. The program began in September 1957

Robert R. Bowie (JD '34), professor of international affairs in the School from 1952 to 1955 and 1957 to 1977 and first director of the Center for International Affairs.

with seven public officials from India, Pakistan, Burma, and Indonesia. Initially, the core of the program consisted of a seminar taught by Professor Mason and a course in economic development taught by Mason, with aid from David Bell and Gustav Papanek. Urged from the outset to take courses in other fields as well, participants were soon accorded the option of becoming degree candidates like other students.

The demand for advice on economic development soon called for organizing additional advisory groups in other countries, and a Development Advisory Service, later reconstituted as the Harvard Institute for International Development, was established. The School meanwhile retained and expanded its training effort. In 1973 the Public Service Fellows were rechristened

Edward S. Mason Fellows. Today the Kennedy School admits annually as Mason Fellows some fifty experienced officials from developing countries.

The GSPA had no monopoly on research or training in international affairs. In the late 1950s the Ford Foundation funded a Center for International Affairs. Its first director was Robert R. Bowie, formerly a professor in the Law School, more recently assistant secretary of state for policy planning in the Eisenhower Administration, now back in the University as a professor in the Government Department. Bowie's Center was located administratively in the Faculty of Arts and Sciences (and physically on the second floor of that faculty's Semitic Museum). Since Bowie planned to sponsor research on current policy issues and also to bring mature public officials to Harvard for advanced study, there were clearly possibilities for competition between his Center and the GSPA. To minimize such competition, Mason and Bowie agreed in September 1957 that the Center would undertake advanced research and provide opportunities for study

and reflection by individuals who were past the training stage. Any training program for younger officials would fall to the GSPA.

Pressure for Change

With a large student population unlike any in the Faculty of Arts and Sciences, and with surging research and advisory efforts extending beyond the conventional boundaries of academic disciplines, it was questionable how long the School could continue to depend for faculty and curriculum nearly exclusively on the two Arts and Sciences departments of Economics and Government.

In 1952 a recently formed Washington Alumni Association recommended that the School develop its own core curriculum, arguing that the GSPA should be more oriented toward professional training. The Association posited that stress on social science disciplines should give way to analysis of current public policy issues. After lively discussion, the GSPA faculty con-

Three Kennedy School deans, Graham Allison, Jr., Edward Mason, and Don Price (far right) join former associate dean and longtime friend of the School, Paul M. Herzog (SB '27) in the classroom named in his honor.

cluded that such a reorientation would be undesirable and rejected the advice. Disciplinary training, they maintained, should not be diluted.

At that time, the School's faculty consisted almost entirely of members of the departments of Economics and Government. Conant urged greater involvement of faculty from the Law School, Business School, and other parts of the University but little resulted. In 1947 Dean Williams had advised him "to recognize frankly that this School is primarily the concern of the departments of Economics and Government."[21] Conant eventually accepted Williams' conclusion. In his final report as Harvard's president, Conant labeled the GSPA an "adjunct" of the Economics and Government departments. "For several years," he wrote, "I presided over the meetings of this faculty and can testify from personal experience as to the complete failure in interfaculty cooperation." He termed this experience his "greatest disappointment as far as the collaboration of several faculties is concerned."[22]

Such criticism led in 1953 to a full-scale review of the School. The Carnegie Corporation provided funding. Paul M. Herzog, a former chairman of the National Labor Relations Board and a longtime member of the GSPA Visiting Committee was named as associate dean to conduct the three-year study.

Issued in January 1957, the Herzog report was generally friendly and sympathetic but criticized emphatically the School's failure to formulate an independent identity. The report attributed this failure primarily to the absence of a curriculum geared specifically to the GSPA's specialized needs. Despite its rich offering of courses, there was no common denominator, no unifying element to give the School the same degree of separateness and cohesion that Harvard's other professional schools enjoyed. "What is required,"

the report contended, "is not less emphasis on public policy issues, but more, with stronger accent in the School's seminars upon issues that are in fact *public* ones."[23] Even the physical plant was censured. Though the Littauer Center had the advantage of bringing all of Harvard's economists and political scientists under one roof, it had distinct disadvantages as well:

Many professors enjoy offices in the building who do not teach in the School's seminars and have no special interest in problems of the public service; many of the students who use the rooms and library every week are not registered in the School or interested in government careers. . . . The point is that, for better or for worse, this arrangement has greatly influenced the School's development and has, like the lack of an independent

Gertrude Manley, registrar from 1953 to 1973, symbolized the School for a generation.

faculty, tended to impair its inchoate character as an independent entity.[24]

The Herzog report recommended a core curriculum of specialized courses in public policy; the naming of a full-time dean; the appointment of a "nucleus faculty," beginning preferably with three professorships filled on different criteria from those of the academic departments; collaboration with Harvard's other professional schools, especially the Law and Business schools; and, finally, a more varied mix of students to include not only mid-career men and women but a number of younger students with intentions of eventually entering public service.

Of the various changes and reforms that the Herzog survey stimulated, none was more quickly adopted than a set of new rules governing faculty appointments. As of 1948 members of the Economics and Government departments had automatically become members of the GSPA faculty for the academic years in which they gave seminars or courses offered by the School. Other faculty were not automatically accorded membership but had

to be voted on by the GSPA faculty. A new policy, proposed by Dean Mason and approved by the faculty in May 1956, put members of the faculties of other departments and professional schools on a par with those of the departments of Economics and Government regarding their selection as members of the GSPA faculty. The qualification for faculty membership became a commitment to teach on a continuing (usually three-year) basis a course or seminar included in the School's curriculum.

Mason also endorsed Herzog's idea of a separate, or nucleus, faculty. Part of his reason for doing so, he admitted, stemmed from rather trivial matters—the difficulty of stimulating attendance at faculty meetings or at weekly student-faculty luncheons, for example. But there

was also a larger problem tied directly to the changing content of disciplines, as reflected in the appointment of faculty, particularly in the Economics Department. When the School was founded in the 1930s, the focus of economics was on fields such as banking, finance, agriculture, and industrial management. By the 1950s the discipline was geared more to economic theory and mathematical economics—fields concerned only secondarily, if at all, with current issues. Mason believed that if new appointments were concentrated in these areas, as seemed likely, it would become increasingly difficult for the Department of Economics to meet its obligations to the GSPA.

Mason questioned whether future faculty who might be unfamiliar with the School and its origins would bother to take an interest in it. The public policy research and training programs on which the School had built its reputation, after all, required considerable inquisitiveness and time and capacity for organized research and training of public officials. He saw no such interest among the more theoretically

Former Canadian Prime Minister Pierre E. Trudeau (AM '46) returned to the School to address a study group.

oriented professors then being appointed in the Government and Economics departments. The solution, Mason argued, was clear:

We should have a small nucleus faculty—three or possibly four members—whose main interests lie in training for the public service and in related research on public policy problems at present not adequately covered. Though their primary allegiance would be to the School, it goes without saying that their academic distinction would be such as to justify membership in the faculties of the participating departments.[25]

Although many faculty members voiced sympathy for Dean Mason's proposal, support was far from unanimous. After lengthy debate, the faculty agreed in December 1956 to a compromise resolution:

It is the sentiment of the Faculty that it welcomes the proposal of the Dean to raise money for three new professorships, to be so established that the major allegiance of those appointed will be to the School. The appointments will be recommended to the Governing Boards by the Faculty of the School, the details for this to be worked out at a later date.[26]

Mason chose to interpret this resolution as a broad endorsement of the idea of a separate faculty. The way was open for a measured step toward the independent School envisioned in the original Littauer gift and the Dodds report. What remained was to raise the funds to make it happen.

While Conant and Herzog were correct in saying that the School had yet to establish an independent identity within the University, "Littauer" had nevertheless acquired an identity in the larger outside world. The very existence of the Washington Alumni Association was testimony. There and all over the world, growing numbers of men and women held Harvard MPA degrees. To cite a few from 1937 to 1957: H. DeWayne Kraeger (1939), chairman of the board of Pacific First Federal Savings and Loan of Seattle; Robert J.M. Matteson (1941), head of the Matteson Associates public consulting firm in Vermont; William D. Carey (1942), executive officer of the American Academy for the Advancement of Science and publisher of *Science* magazine; David L. Grove (1942), president of the U.S. Council on International Business; Paul Ylvisaker (1945), one-time vice president of the Ford Foundation and dean of the Harvard School of Education; Robert C. Wood (1948), secretary of HUD under President Johnson and subsequently president of the University of Massachusetts and superintendent of schools in Boston; Anthony M. Solomon (1948), president of the Federal Reserve Bank in New York; Senator William Proxmire (1949); Lyman Hamilton (1949), subsequently president of ITT; General John Wickham (1955), chief of staff of the U.S. Army; Ravi Inder Gulhati(1956), director of the economics department of the World Bank; Minos Andreas Zombanakis (1957), chairman of INA International Holdings in London; Franco Alfredo Grassini (1957), head of Fiat do Brasil;

and Aftab Ahmad Khan (1958), secretary of the Ministry of Defense of Pakistan. Among those who received master's degrees for their studies at the School during those years were Pierre Eliot Trudeau, subsequently prime minister of Canada; Congressman Hamilton Fish, Jr.; and Paul Volcker, head of the Federal Reserve system.

For many alumni, seminars and more informal gatherings in the Littauer building had served as molding experiences, turning their careers in new directions. *Public Policy* and monographs issuing from School research programs extended still more broadly the influence of the School's faculty. Although much was to come in the future, much had already been accomplished.

3 Metamorphosis

At the end of the 1957–58 academic year, following eleven years of service, Edward S. Mason stepped down as dean of the Graduate School of Public Administration. As his successor, President Nathan Pusey went outside the Harvard faculties to name Don K. Price, then a vice president of the Ford Foundation.

For Price, becoming GSPA dean meant not merely a change of jobs but the beginning of a new career. He was a 1931 graduate of Vanderbilt University and a former Rhodes Scholar. While in college he had been a reporter for the *Nashville Evening Tennessean*; after graduation he worked for a variety of public and private agencies, including the Social Science Research Council, the Bureau of the Budget, the Hoover Commission on governmental reorganization, and the Defense Department's Research and Development Board. In 1953 he joined the Ford Foundation and soon became supervisor of grants for overseas development. In that capacity he worked closely with Dean Mason in setting up the Pakistan and Iran pro-grams. He eventually concluded, however, that foundation work did not suit him and began casting about for a new job. When the Harvard offer came along, he readily accepted.

Condition of the School

Although a newcomer to Harvard, Price knew the GSPA from his work with the Ford Foundation. He was aware that the School still lacked a place and mission within the larger University. While interviewing Price for the deanship, Pusey confided that he had given some thought to closing the School and would in fact do so unless Price established more clearly why it should stand as an apparent equal of well-focused faculties such as Business, Law, and Medicine, all preeminent in the professions they served. It was on a "make-it-or-break-it" basis that Price accepted his new job.[27]

To a considerable extent, the School's difficulties stemmed directly from its exceedingly ambitious general conception. Among

schools of its kind, it ranked as one of the most progressive and innovative. It stressed substantive aspects of public policy rather than public administration. Price, who had some responsiblity for administrative management techniques while at the Bureau of the Budget, believed that the School carried this emphasis a bit far, almost to the point of ignoring questions of how government actually conducted its affairs. Nonetheless, he preferred error on that side to the error of overemphasizing routine mechanics and processes of administration.

More worrisome to Price was the absence of a curriculum clearly distinct from those of the Economics and Government departments. Without a special training program clearly professional in orientation, Price could not easily answer Pusey's implicit question as to why Harvard should pretend to have a professional school concerned with public service.

The focus on public policy as opposed to administration imposed a requirement for a large and diverse faculty. Yet the School was perennially short of money. Since 1937

the endowment of the University as a whole increased by 133 percent; that of the School had increased only 13 percent. Given the growing demands on the School over the years and the erosion in the value of its endowment due to inflation, the GSPA had little financial capacity for rising to opportunities. Pusey promised Price that he would make an effort to shore up the School's endowment, but made clear that his concern for restoring the health of the Divinity School took precedence.

Fully cognizant of the handicaps, Price moved slowly. He used the Herzog report as a primary guide. Of the report's many recommendations, he acted first on the one to provide the School with a nucleus faculty. The process began with his own appointment as the School's first full-

time dean. The following year David E. Bell, who had been instrumental in assisting Dean Mason in setting up the Pakistan and Iran projects, was appointed as secretary. Previous secretaries had customarily been junior members of the Government Department clearly in the running for tenure. Among them had been Charles E. Cherington, Robert G. McCloskey, and Arthur Maass, all of whom had later become professors in that department. Bell was the first economist to be named secretary. Although Bell held an appointment in the Economics Department, Price's intent was that Bell's primary affiliation be with the Faculty of Public Administration. After Bell's departure from Harvard in 1961 to become director of the Bureau of the Budget in Washington, the post of secretary went to the University's first professor of public administration, John D. Montgomery. A professor in the Government Department, specializing in political aspects of national development, Montgomery, too, met Price's criterion of being affiliated primarily with the School.

The creation of professorships

John D. Montgomery (AM '48, Ph.D. '51), first professor of public administration, from 1963 to the present.

solely within the Faculty of Public Administration hinged on additional financing. The original net endowment of $1.5 million left no leeway for faculty appointments. By 1953 the endowment had risen to slightly less than $1.6 million, with a credit balance of $210,000. Ten years later these figures had approximately doubled—the endowment stood at $3.26 million and the credit balance at nearly $400,000. Approximately one-third of the increase in the available resources came from the School's share of a 1960 Ford Foundation grant to the University for international studies. The rest came through small gifts, none larger than $2,000, and miscellaneous savings from various sources.[28]

These increases, Price believed, enabled the School to begin planning additional permanent faculty appointments. However, as he conceded in his fifth report as dean, published in 1963, he saw no point in doing so given the GSPA's basic structure and curriculum:

As long as our seminars and courses are so thoroughly intertwined with those of other Faculties, and partic-

ularly of the Departments of Economics and Government of the Faculty of Arts and Sciences, it is an asset for a member of the Faculty of Public Administration to have a teaching role in some other Faculty as well. . . . But the process of considering the selection of appointments from the point of view of this School, and in consideration of its special purposes, has done much to help the School develop a sense of its own unique purpose and place among the Harvard Faculties.[29]

In other words, the School was finding a niche, but it did not seem likely to evolve into an independent institution, on a footing with Harvard's other professional schools. That the situation would change in the near future probably seemed as unlikely to Price as to anyone.

The Kennedy Memorial

Conant, Pusey, Mason, Price, and others wanted Harvard to develop an effective center for public service training in part because of their shared belief that the government's business was becoming both more important and more complex. Each had considerable interest in government affairs. During World War II Conant had played a major role in the Manhattan Project, which produced the atomic bomb. Afterward he had been consulted by Washington on many issues arising from the cold war, especially the emerging nuclear and thermonuclear arms competition with the Soviet Union. He left the presidency of Harvard to succeed John J. McCloy as America's representative in the new Federal Republic of Germany. Mason's many roles in government were mentioned earlier. Though Pusey's own career had been entirely in academe, first as a teacher of classics and, before coming to Harvard, as president of Lawrence College, he believed strongly in the duty of universities to provide national leadership. In

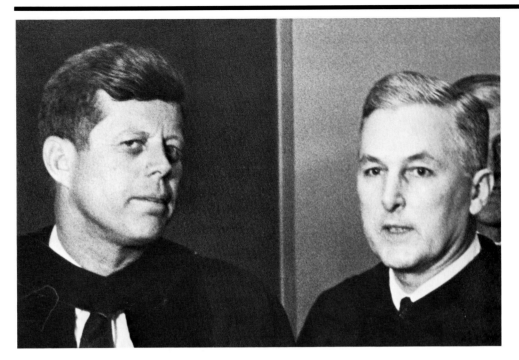

President John F. Kennedy (BS '40) and Harvard President Nathan M. Pusey (AB '28, AM '32, Ph.D. '37, LLD '72 hon.).

Then Senator John F. Kennedy (BS '40) with Cardinal Cushing at Harvard's 1959 commencement.

the immediate foreground of Price's appointment was the nationwide uproar resulting from *Sputnik*—the Soviet Union's apparent demonstration of superiority in rocketry and perhaps in other branches of science. One of Price's many credentials for the deanship was his expertise in the new roles played in government by scientists and engineers. In 1954 he had published *Government and Science,* and in 1965 he would issue his penetrating and still unrivalled study *The Scientific Estate.* In an era of thermonuclear weapons and intercontinental missiles, as well as of almost unparalleled economic and political change, it seemed more imperative than ever that the nation's best minds address issues of public policy.

In 1960 John Fitzgerald Kennedy was elected president of the United States. In his administration many observers saw evidence that the nation's best and brightest were answering the call to duty. This feeling was particularly strong at Harvard, for Kennedy was a graduate of the College (1940) and recently an overseer and member of the GSPA Visit-

Professor Archibald Cox (AB '34, LLB '37, LLD '75 hon.), President Kennedy's solicitor general and later special prosecutor in the Watergate proceedings.

ing Committee. He had drawn on the Harvard faculty for campaign advice (even if he accepted less of it than most of the advisers believed), and he included some Harvard notables in his administration, among them Arts and Sciences Dean McGeorge Bundy as special assistant for national security affairs; economist Carl Kaysen as Bundy's deputy; historian Arthur Schlesinger, Jr. as another White House aide; David Bell as director of the Bureau of the Budget; economist John Kenneth Galbraith as ambassador to India; and law professor Archibald Cox as solicitor general.

For millions, the young and charismatic Kennedy personified a new generation in American political life. Kennedy's example vitalized interest in politics and government across the nation. At Harvard it aroused new, strong interest in the Graduate School of Public Administration.

What happened next is inseparable from what happened in planning for a Kennedy Library. Early in Kennedy's presidency, Pusey approached Kennedy about depositing his papers at Harvard or in an easily accessible place nearby. The precedent for establishing such a presidential library outside of Washington had been set by FDR, Truman, and Eisenhower. "We . . . felt," Pusey recalled, "that he [President Kennedy] would probably be reelected, serve a second term, and then go out of office as a relatively young man. We thought it not unlikely that he would like to have an office in the Library and live in this community which he loved and where he had so many friends. Perhaps we'd make a professor out of him before we got through. This is what we were dreaming about."[30]

After an exchange of correspondence, Kennedy and Pusey met in June 1961 in the White House Oval Office. Kennedy had just returned from an unproductive summit meeting in Vienna with Soviet Premier Nikita Khrushchev. It was obvious to Pusey that Kennedy's mind was on matters far distant from the Library. At one point in the conversation, Pusey remembered, Kennedy even mentioned that it might be preferable to locate the Library somewhere else, near his home in Hyannis Port or in Palm Beach, for example. Pusey was shocked, but by the end of the meeting he believed that Kennedy was firm about putting the Library near Harvard. "It was perfectly clear," Pusey said later, "he had thought his way through the problem and that he personally had come to favor the idea of having his Library close to Harvard, that is, close to Widener Library."[31] After further correspondence, it was announced from the White House on November 10, 1961, that President Kennedy was seriously looking at plans for the establishment of a library-museum for the permanent deposit of his official papers and other materials, to be located near Cambridge, built with private funds, and operated by the U.S. National Archives.

In the spring of 1963 Kennedy visited Boston to survey several possible sites for the proposed library-

President John F. Kennedy (BS '40) visits Boston in 1961 to review sites for the Presidential Library on a parcel of land adjacent to the Business School.

Senator Robert F. Kennedy (BA '48) headed the John F. Kennedy Memorial Library Corporation from 1963 until his death in 1968. Here seen with Jacqueline Kennedy and Michael Forrestal (JD '53).

museum complex. After considering alternatives, he selected a site on the Boston side of the Charles River just off Western Avenue. On September 30, 1963, he approved a memorandum of understanding with Harvard, agreeing to locate the Library on this site, provided that no more attractive spot became available.

After Kennedy's assassination in Dallas on November 22, 1963, the Kennedy family indicated a wish to carry out this plan. In December 1963 articles of organization were filed in Massachusetts to create a John F. Kennedy Memorial Library Corporation as the fundraising body to build the Library. The head of the corporation was the late president's brother, Robert F. Kennedy. Later that same month a group of the president's former associates and advisers, including many who were or had been on the Harvard faculty, met over dinner in Washington to discuss what might be done to perpetuate Kennedy's memory. All agreed that in addition to an archive and museum, it would be fitting to include some kind of "living" center or institute, honoring Kennedy's interest in politics and government

The "little yellow house" at 78 Mt. Auburn St., the original home of the Institute of Politics, from 1966 to 1978.

and emphasizing the practical side of public policy. As to what exactly the center should do, opinions differed. Some favored an institute devoted to study and research; others preferred more actual problem-solving. Afterward, many who attended the dinner wrote their suggestions, which Arthur Schlesinger, Jr. forwarded to Robert Kennedy. Though there was still no consensus on the proposed institute's function, nearly all agreed that it should be administered independently of either the Library or Harvard and operated by its own board of trustees.

Pusey, still eager to locate the Kennedy Library at Harvard, was uneasy over the possibility of a research or policy center situated at Harvard but operating with no University oversight. He eventually persuaded the Kennedy family that Harvard could run the proposed institute more effectively than could a group from outside. At a June 1964 meeting he reached an understanding with Robert Kennedy that the institute would become part of the GSPA, with the entire school then to stand as the Kennedy memorial.

Departing from longstanding precedent, the University would create a John F. Kennedy School of Government. This arrangement would ensure permanency for the institute as an integral part of the University. At the same time, the School of Public Administration would be rededicated to the appropriate purpose of encouraging the application of trained intelligence to the solution of public problems.

Later that summer Don Price and Robert Kennedy arrived at an informal agreement that spelled out what would be done. The institute would become "the second major part" of the Kennedy School, the GSPA being the first. Like Robert Bowie's Center for International Affairs in the Faculty of Arts and Sciences, the institute would grant no degrees and give no courses for aca-

demic credit. Rather, it would focus on promoting advanced research among those interested in or engaged in politics and political affairs. It would also arrange conferences, lectureships, study seminars, and other programs outside conventional academic confines. Finally, it would be responsible for conducting extracurricular programs designed to attract and involve Harvard undergraduates in practical politics and public service. Responsibility for administering these programs would fall to the institute's director, who would also be given the title of associate dean of the School.[32]

The director would receive an appointment from the University after the institute came into being, but it was understood from the beginning that the post would be filled by Richard E. Neustadt. A professor of government at Columbia University who had served in the Truman Administration and been an occasional consultant to the Kennedy White House, Neustadt was enthusiastically approved by the Kennedy family. As the author of *Presidential Power*, a pathbreaking study of the American presidency, Neustadt re-

The October 17, 1966, meeting formally establishing the Institute of Politics as a living memorial to the late president and changing the name of the School from the Graduate School of Public Administration to the John F. Kennedy School of Government. Seated at the table from left: Dean Don K. Price (AM '58 hon., LLD '70 hon.), the Hon. Averill Harriman, Michael V. Forrestal (JD '53), and Richard Neustadt (AM '42, Ph.D. '51). The portrait by William F. Draper of President Kennedy, shown here, now hangs in the Forum of the Kennedy School.

ceived an equally enthusiastic welcome into the Harvard Department of Government. Moreover, he was familiar with the GSPA's origins and purpose, having done his graduate work before World War II in the joint Program in Political Economy and Government. In January 1965 his appointment became official, along with the announcement by Harvard that formal creation of an Institute of Politics (IOP) would follow immediately upon receipt of a $10 million endowment for it from the Kennedy Library Corporation. In December, as a first major step, the Ford Foundation pledged $2 million and an anonymous donor gave an additional $500,000. The Institute began its program in the fall of 1966.

The Big Plan and Its Demise

Out of the decision to create the IOP evolved the so-called Big Plan to enlarge the Library into a complex of buildings housing not only the museum and presidential archives, but academic and research facilities

as well. Included would be the Institute of Politics, an international studies building to house the Center for International Affairs, and a new and larger Littauer Center to alleviate the growing congestion in the old center on Kirkland Street and to keep the School of Government and the IOP physically as close together as possible, with the Economics and Government departments also nearby. In view of the increased demand for space, the Library Corporation's architect I.M. Pei recommended relocating the Library in Cambridge on a twelve-acre site at the corner of Memorial Drive and Boylston Street, where the MBTA (the Boston subway system) currently had its car barns. President Kennedy had also inquired about this location during his trip to Boston in 1963 but was told at the

time that it was unavailable. In the aftermath of the assassination, with emotions running strong, the Cambridge City Council adopted a resolution endorsing the project. Later that year the Massachusetts General Court passed special legislation clearing the way—or so it seemed at the time—for the MBTA to vacate the property and transfer title to the U.S. Government and Kennedy Library Corporation.

Except for the international studies building, for which he had money in hand, Pusey was reluctant to commit Harvard. He had two concerns. One was that local sensitivities to Harvard might cause the city of Cambridge to withdraw its support in mid-stream. The second was that the Big Plan would require fundraising that would detract from other projects high on the univer-

Richard E. Neustadt (AM '42, Ph.D. '52), first director of the Institute of Politics, and Mrs. Katherine Graham, publisher of the *Washington Post* and member of the Senior Advisory Committee, at the October 17, 1966, meeting.

sity's agenda, as, for example, an up-to-date undergraduate science center.

Slowly, Pusey's resistance wore down. Neustadt, Price, and others argued that the Big Plan was essential to the goal of establishing close Institute-School relations and thereby using the Institute's resources to help improve the quality of the School. If the two were forced to live apart, it was hardly likely that the marriage would ever prove a success. Members of the Kennedy family, in particular Robert Kennedy, communicated to Pusey their own high enthusiasm. "This makes so much sense," Robert Kennedy remarked at one point, "that I can't bear not to see it done."[33] In June 1966, in an exchange of letters with Pusey, the Library Corporation agreed to proceed with fundraising for the IOP endowment while Harvard pledged

to take appropriate legal action to rename the School of Public Administration, acquire 2.2 acres of land on the memorial site, and participate so far as practicable in the Big Plan concept, beginning with construction of the international studies building. And, Pusey added, "if we can manage it, we also hope to move the entire program now conducted in Littauer to this place." It was a tentative commitment, to be sure, but, considering Pusey's earlier opposition, a major concession.[34]

The exchange of letters between Robert Kennedy and Nathan Pusey in June 1966 officially brought the Library Corporation and Harvard into partnership to reinvigorate the School and give it a new home. The two goals were intertwined. Relocating the School meant escaping the increasingly cramped quarters

of the building on Kirkland Street. More important it meant acquiring a site physically separate from the Economics and Government departments. Associating the Kennedy School with the new Institute of Politics would have a catalytic effect in generating a new curriculum.

The rest of the Big Plan proved infeasible and not so essential after all. The MBTA experienced trouble finding a suitable alternative location for its facilities. As time passed, the city of Cambridge developed doubts. In deference to complaints by residents—some of them members of the Harvard faculty—about the many tourists the Library's museum was expected to attract, a new city manager blocked the start of construction.

Added to these difficulties were Harvard's own problems of gauging the cost of its participation and finding the necessary funds. As of spring 1969 Pusey estimated Harvard's share of the total cost of the project at $20 million, less than a quarter of which had been raised. By this time, the war in Vietnam had become a focus of student and faculty protest against the government and often

Evolving designs for the John Fitzgerald Kennedy Library-museum complex. 1965, 1970, and 1974.

against universities themselves. April 1969 saw student demonstrators occupy University Hall. At Pusey's request, police removed the demonstrators. A large-scale student strike ensued. The succeeding two years brought frequent turmoil to the University and to Cambridge.

By the 1970s the emotional reaction to President Kennedy's death had faded. With construction of the Kennedy Library threatened to be delayed for years, the Library Corporation announced in February 1975 that it would look elsewhere for a suitable location. It eventually opted for a site on Columbia Point in Dorchester, near the new Boston campus of the University of Massachusetts. The Kennedy School of Government thus lost the Library along with its attendant opportunities but by a happy irony thus preserved sufficient space eventually to have offices and classrooms comparable to those of other Harvard professional schools.

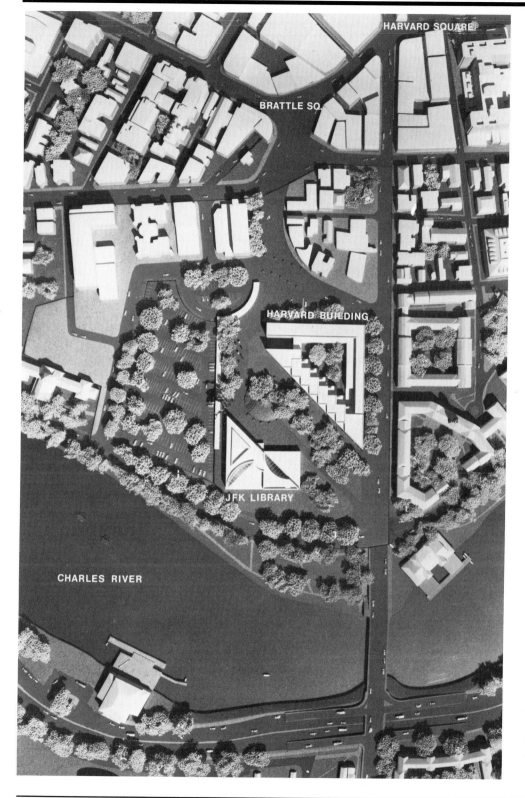

HARVARD SQUARE

BRATTLE SQ.

HARVARD BUILDING

JFK LIBRARY

CHARLES RIVER

The Price-Neustadt Collaboration

In the 1950s Dean Mason had reviewed the argument that the School needed a curriculum of its own. The departments of Economics and Government, he had warned, were growing increasingly abstract and remote from operational problems, just as the disciplines attained higher precision. By the 1960s this was even more apparent, as government made increasing use of systems analysis and other analytic methodologies not commonly included in academic social science.

Price had perceived from the outset the desirability of new courses, if not a new curriculum. One of his early innovations was a Seminar in Science and Public Policy. Funded by the Rockefeller Foundation, it linked the School with the Engineering faculty, where approaches such as systems analysis were comparatively more familiar. With the creation of the Kennedy School and the arrival of Neustadt, Price could begin to think in larger terms.

Price and Neustadt reinforced one

'HALLS OF IVY'

1961 cartoon reflects President Kennedy's appointments of Harvardians to his administration.

another. Shrewd, patient, and self-effacing, Price lived by the maxim that a man can accomplish a great deal if he will let other people take the credit. Thus it pleased him to see advances by the new Kennedy School attributed to the Kennedy family or one of their associates or to President Pusey or to one member or another of the faculty. Indeed, he encouraged this.

Neustadt, too, preferred the orchestra pit to the stage. His book *Presidential Power* had examined ways in which politicians achieved results. Much of it illustrated a point made by Harry Truman as he was leaving the White House. Pointing to his chair, Truman said of the president-elect, General Eisenhower, "Ike will sit here, and he'll say 'Do this' and 'Do that,' and nothing will happen." In politics, Neustadt ar-

gued, leadership is exercised by persuasion, not command. The key to getting a result is to mobilize people who want that result for reasons of their own. In Neustadt's view, a university was a political arena. His principle held for Cambridge as well as Washington. Together, he and Price put it into practice.

Making the most of his status as a newcomer needing orientation, Neustadt day after day lunched or had coffee or drinks with one faculty member, then another. One of his conditions for coming to Harvard had been a residence within walking distance. (Columbia had provided him that in New York.) In a house at 10 Traill Street, Neustadt and his wife Bert entertained small groups from Harvard and the larger world. Theirs were Washington-style dinner parties (Capitol Hill, not Embassy Row)—informal, always fun, but never purposeless.

Neustadt was looking for faculty members with two characteristics. First, they had to exhibit some concern with practice as well as theory. It had to be neither a short-term nor pride-driven concern to give advice on current decisions, but a longer-

term concern with the way governmental decisions could be made and implemented. The frame of mind Neustadt sought was that which former Dean Mason had exemplified in his conclusion that training such as that for Public Service Fellows was a precondition for economic development in less-developed lands. A second criterion, at least as important to Neustadt, was that the professors possess unquestioned distinction in their faculties or disciplines. Nothing could more quickly doom the new Kennedy School than to be perceived as a haven for the not quite successful. The School could accommodate misfits but not second-raters.

Gradually, Neustadt identified a core group of faculty members meeting his criteria. Carl Kaysen of the Economics Department was one of the first chosen but soon left Harvard to succeed J. Robert Oppenheimer as head of the Institute for Advanced Study in Princeton. The member of the Economics Department who entered the circle and remained was Thomas C. Schelling, a game theorist whose previous work had had great impact on governmen-

tal thinking about nuclear warfare. Howard Raiffa, one of the pioneers of mathematical decision and bargaining theory, provided a link with the Business School. Also from the Business School faculty was Joseph Bower, an innovative student of business strategy. The Law School was represented by Philip Heymann, a specialist in criminal justice. Frederick Mosteller, a professor of statistics, became one of the inner group. Others on the periphery included economists Richard Caves, Otto Eckstein, and Martin Feldstein and historian Ernest May.

Another point in *Presidential Power* was that successful politicians kept open as many options as possible for as long as possible. Price and Neustadt applied this principle as well. Though hoarding money for the day when it could be used for curriculum development, Neustadt immediately made the IOP one of Harvard's liveliest and most prominent elements. It gained automatic visibility from its prestigious Senior Advisory Committee headed by W. Averell Harriman, which took its duties seriously and paid frequent visits to the yellow frame house at 78 Mt. Auburn Street where the Institute began its life. Among the Committee's members were Robert Kennedy, President Kennedy's widow Jacqueline, *Washington Post* publisher Katharine Graham, former Secretary of Defense Robert A. Lovett and incumbent Robert McNamara, former Secretary of the Treasury C. Douglas Dillon, Senator John Sherman Cooper of Kentucky, and Senator Henry M. Jackson of Washington. Neustadt brought in a sequence of Resident Fellows, including *Washington Post* columnist David Broder; voting rights activist Vernon Jordan, later to be head of the Urban League; Sir Eric Roll, formerly permanent undersecretary of state in the Department of Economic Affairs in London; and, to be bipartisan as well as international, former Eisenhower staff assistant Stephen Hess and Jonathan Moore, earlier legislative assistant to Senator Leverett Saltonstall and more recently an official in the Defense Department, then State (eventually to return as director of the IOP). Neustadt also brought to Cambridge for short-term, off-the-record visits figures such as Congressman Gerald Ford and John Lindsay, then mayor of New York. One such invitation proved a mistake. Secretary of Defense Robert McNamara became the target of a large antiwar demonstration and had to be escorted to safety through Harvard's underground steam tunnels. The student guiding him was Barney Frank, now a congressman from Massachusetts.

In other ways besides bringing to Cambridge renowned politicians, Neustadt made the IOP a magnet

Institute of Politics Director Jonathan Moore (MPA '57).

"the May group." The rapporteur, providing "creative minutes," was Neustadt's Ph.D. student, Graham Allison. If all else failed, at least the Kennedy School could become a Brookings on the Charles.

for undergraduates and other students considering such careers for themselves. Non-credit study groups were organized around topics such as the nuts and bolts of campaigning, political journalism, and problems in contemporary domestic and foreign policy. Study group leaders included not only Institute Fellows but members of the state legislature and the local press corps.

These connections with the outside world and with the College would benefit an independent professional school, if that dream materialized. They also provided a base on which to fall back if the dream faded. Not unimportantly, all this activity helped reassure donors to the Kennedy memorial that *something* was happening.

Yet another activitiy managed by Neustadt was the quiet development

of a research agenda. Every Saturday morning he met with members of his prospective core faculty and with others, including officials who journeyed from Washington for solace or for counsel. This larger group included Francis Bator, an economist, then deputy national security assistant to President Johnson, soon to be a professor in the School; former Pentagon whiz kid Harry Rowen, then at the Bureau of the Budget, later to be professor at the Stanford Business School; M.I.T. political scientists Fred Iklé and William W. Kaufmann; Harvard Law School professors Adam Yarmolinsky and John McNaughton, the latter on leave at the Defense Department; and McNaughton's assistant, political scientist Morton Halperin. At Neustadt's request, May served as chairman of what came to be known as

A New Curriculum

Formal discussion of a new curriculum commenced in the fall of 1967 when Professor Montgomery raised the question of revamping the School's doctoral programs. He suggested using the nearly dormant Doctor of Public Administration degree to accommodate the special needs of students who wanted to prepare for a government rather than academic career. Though this suggestion garnered little support, faculty discussion through the winter generated some enthusiasm for a wholly new doctoral program that would combine either economics or political science with professional studies in law, business, medicine, public health, or city planning.[35]

During the spring and summer of

1968, Price sounded out opinions, especially among the barons of the Economics and Government departments and the deans of other professional schools. Derek Bok, dean of the Law School, proved particularly receptive. Himself a specialist in labor law, trained in economics as well as law, and the son-in-law of economist-diplomats Gunnar and Alva Myrdal, Bok liked the proposal in principle. In addition, he was aware that the decade of the 1960s was bringing to the Law School increasing numbers of students who wanted to work in the public sector and who criticized the Law School's own third-year electives as being narrow and sterile. A new Kennedy School program could help to solve his problem.

At the time, Bok was collaborating with John T. Dunlop on a book entitled *Labor and the American Community.* As chairman of Harvard's Economics Department during the first half of the 1960s, Dunlop had helped raise money for professorships to hold joint appointments between Arts and Sciences and professional schools. One of the leading labor mediators in the nation, he was a living link between the academic world and the world of public affairs. He was later the dean of the Faculty of Arts and Sciences and for a period in the 1970s, secretary of labor. Dunlop had long supported and contributed to the Public Administration program. Also, he happened to have known Neustadt since the late 1940s, when Neustadt did staff work for a Taft-Hartley Board of Inquiry on coal of which Dunlop was a member. Although more recognized for the moment for a study of how the Faculty of Arts and Sciences could attract and retain new faculty, Dunlop also encouraged Price.

Neustadt's preparatory work was about to pay off. In mid-April 1968 he circulated tentative proposals. Included were suggestions for a new curriculum and new degrees to take

Ernest May (AM '59 hon.), Charles Warren Professor of History, points out the historical dimension.

Professor Richard E. Neustadt (AM '42, Ph.D. '51), former associate dean and director of the Institute of Politics, has been associated with the School since 1965.

advantage of the opportunities he saw, as well as an outline of the help that could be expected from the personnel and other resources of the IOP. Listening carefully to reactions, Neustadt set aside the summer to draft a document that could win support from a substantial number of Arts and Sciences and professional school faculty.

The summer's effort to make the necessary refinements spanned the continent. As befitted the season, Neustadt chose to work informally and often relied on others to flesh out the details. Among those deeply involved were Raiffa and Allison, soon to be junior members of the Government Department, both of whom were spending the summer at the Rand Corporation in California, and two other juniors working in Cambridge, economists Richard Zeckhauser and Henry Jacoby. With

their contributions and advice from others, particularly Bok and Dunlop, Neustadt's plan progressed. By the end of summer there existed a general plan for a program with three elements—a doctoral degree in political economy; a new master's in political economy degree; and a modification of the existing master's program to accommodate students in law and medicine.

During the fall of 1968 this proposed program ran into criticism from professors who had not been part of Neustadt's summer circle. Some in the Government Department had misgivings about a Ph.D. in "applied" political science. Some in the Economics Department felt that there was no need for any new degrees; their existing M.A. and Ph.D. programs could do it all. Price and Neustadt managed eventually to allay most concerns among fellow members of the Government Department, and Dunlop saw to it that the economists did not interpose road blocks. In November 1968 the proposed new program won approval from the Committee on Educational Policy (then, in effect, the steering committee) of the Faculty of Arts

and Sciences. On December 3, 1968, that Faculty then gave formal approval to creation of a Committee on Higher Degrees in Public Policy. The minutes of that meeting show Price's responses to the questions that still troubled some of his colleagues:

A question was raised as to why this Faculty should award the degree and not the Kennedy School. Professor Price responded that a large proportion of the students at the doctoral level in this joint program will want to be prepared to teach as well as do research and for that the Ph.D., rather than the Doctor of Public Administration, is a prerequisite. The situation is quite parallel to the Ph.D. in Medical Sciences or in Education, or for that matter in Political Economy and Government, which for so long has been a basis of collaboration between the Kennedy School and this Faculty. The President explained further that the Faculty of Arts and Sciences was the only Faculty authorized to award the Ph.D. degree.

For the Kennedy School, it was a stroke of luck that the necessary legislation reached the floor of the

Richard Zeckhauser (AB '62, Ph.D. '69), professor of political economy, chairman of the School's Research Committee, and director of the Faculty Project on Regulation.

Faculty of Arts and Sciences when and as it did. The war in Vietnam had already become a target of large protest meetings. Other universities had suffered disruption; Columbia, for example, had closed briefly during the preceding spring because of clashes between students and police. At Harvard tension increased as a result of agitation by some students and faculty for abolition of ROTC. It was therefore not a propitious time for conservative faculty members to oppose the University's providing training for public service. On the other hand, the issues might never have come to a vote if postponed beyond December 3, for the next faculty meeting was, in fact, disrupted by demonstration. Subsequent meetings were dominated by questions of whether or how the demonstrators were to be disciplined. Then came spring, the occupation of University

Hall, and two years of seldom rational turbulence.

With the formal vote of December 3, Price, Neustadt, and their collaborators were free to proceed. Dunlop became chairman of the new Committee on Higher Degrees. The other members were Dean Bok of the Law School; Robert Ebert of the Medical School; economist Francis Bator, newly appointed as a professor in the Kennedy School; James Duesenberry of the Economics Department; Mosteller; Raiffa; and Neustadt. During the spring and summer of 1969, work progressed on core courses for the new master's program: microeconomic theory to be taught by Schelling; quantitative analysis by Mosteller; decision theory by Raiffa; and political analysis by Neustadt. Zeckhauser, Allison, and Jacoby also continued to be deeply involved. By the fall of 1969, the Kennedy School had its first class of candidates for the Master of Public Policy degree. Of the twenty-one students admitted to the program in its first year, five were also candidates for a medical degree, five for a law degree, and one for a Master's in Business Administration.

Faculty Changes

It was an obvious corollary that the faculty of the new Kennedy School should be different in composition from the faculty of the earlier Graduate School of Public Administration. But there was no rush. Neither Price nor Neustadt nor Bok nor Dunlop saw reason to provoke unnecessary debate.

It soon became evident that the new program involved details of no interest to faculty members outside of the enterprise. In 1969 the faculty gladly agreed to the creation of a new committee structure that included a general Executive Committee and three specialized committees, with each of the latter assigned responsibility for a specific part of the School's program—one to direct the Public Policy Program, another to oversee the Mid-Career Program, and a third to serve as a faculty advisory and planning body for the IOP. A fourth committee, known simply as the Faculty Committee, operated as the faculty's general agent for the review and guidance of its affairs; in practice this usually

Robert J. Murray (MPA '67), former under secretary of the Navy, directs the National Security Program in the School.

meant taking final action on all appointments other than those involving permanent tenure.

Though there was no doubt in Dean Price's mind that further change was necessary and unavoidable, he hesitated to press the matter. "I have been reluctant to recognize this issue," he told his colleagues, "lest I seem unappreciative of the help and cooperation the School has received from many professors whose primary interests lie in other directions."[36] What prompted him to act was an initiative from Bok who in 1971 had succeeded Pusey as president of the University. Referring to the Watergate scandals then coming to light in Washington, Bok declared in 1973 that the recent "dolorous record" of government called for corrective action by American institutions of higher learning. As Harvard's contribution, he announced that he would personally chair a committee for the development of a university-wide Program in Public Policy and Administration, with the aim of helping to restore the public's trust and confidence in its civil servants. "What is needed," Bok argued in out-

lining his plans for the program, "is nothing less than the education of a new profession."[37] He further announced that as part of a new fund-raising campaign for the University, he would give special attention to strengthening the Kennedy School's endowment.

In view of these new circumstances, Price proposed in December 1974 that the faculty reorganize itself, with membership divided into four categories:

(a) those full professors whose permanent tenure is wholly or partly the School's responsibility, who are willing to accept their full share of the School's academic and administrative responsibilities;

(b) those professors, associate professors, and assistant professors who are now on the School's budget for fixed

terms, for half or more of their salaries;

(c) professors of all ranks (and lecturers) to be invited by the faculty to join its membership for a term of years while teaching courses or conducting research determined by the faculty to be of continuing importance to its purposes as a professional responsibility for the School's activities. (To make up the initial roster, this category should include automatically all those teaching courses developed for the School's purposes and carried in whole or in part on the School's budget.)

(d) a limited number of additional faculty members to be designated annually by the dean in accord with past practice. (This procedure would be used to include, in strictly limited numbers, those who are in a position to contribute to the School's program by virtue of their administrative positions or their scholarly interests.)[38]

Henry Cisneros (MPA '73), mayor of San Antonio.

Though the proposed changes engendered much discussion, real opposition was minimal. The motion passed unanimously, to become effective the following academic year. At that time the faculty dropped from ninety-eight to thirty-seven members. With the subsequent growth in the School, this core faculty soon rose to over seventy members, but it was by then a separate faculty teaching courses designed specifically for the School's students.

When Price left the deanship in 1977, it was with the knowledge that he had helped the School contribute to the education of hundreds of students. A list of even fewer than from the earlier period, all MPAs, includes Ambassador Arthur Okun (1959); Luis F. de O Penna (1962), president of Letra S.A. of Rio de Janeiro; President Miguel de la Madrid-Hurtado of Mexico (1965); Senator Larry Pressler (1966); Edwin A. Deagle (1966), a senior adviser at the Rockefeller Foundation; Representative James Moody, Jr. (1967); Robert J. Murray (1967), under secretary of the Navy in the 1970s and subsequently director of national security studies in the Kennedy School; Clive Priestly (1968), under secretary in the Cabinet Office in London; Elsa Porter (1971), assistant secretary of commerce in the Carter Administration; Henry Cisneros (1973), mayor of San Antonio; Meyer Frucher (1974), president of Battery Park City; Ira Jackson (1976), commissioner of revenue for Massachusetts; and Philip Johnston (1977), director of human resources for Massachusetts. Unlike his predecessors, Price also had the satisfaction of having overseen the School's transition. Though still small in size and financially poor, it had now become an independent professional school with its own character and identity.

Emergence

In describing his first year as dean, Graham T. Allison, Jr. likened his experience to that of the Abbe Sieyè's who, when questioned about what he had done during the French Revolution, replied: "I survived." "The School, on the other hand," he added, ". . . has done a little better."[39] Indeed, by the end of that first year, it had clearly broken out of its cocoon and was approaching flight.

Allison quickly became accustomed to his new responsibilities. Harvard's youngest dean, assuming the post at age thirty-seven, had previously served as the School's associate dean and as chairman of its Public Policy Program. A graduate of Harvard College, like Price, he and Mason augmented their education with two years at Oxford, in Allison's case as a Marshall Scholar studying philosophy, politics, and economics. In the academic world he won almost overnight acclaim for *Essence of Decision*, published in 1972. A pathbreaking analysis of the Cuban missile crisis, it identified three alternative models, or conceptual lenses, that could be used in explaining governmental behavior.

Model I focuses on the purposive acts of unified governments; Model II highlights the organizations of which a government consists and their standard operating procedures; and Model III spotlights individual players in positions and the bureaucratic politics among them from which choices emerge. "Allison's Model I, Model II, and Model III" became standard terms in political science, so much so that a review of the debate about these ideas could be titled "Allison's Wonderland."[40] The new dean was also involved in government, especially in foreign affairs, as a consultant to the Department of Defense and the Rand Corporation, an International Affairs Fellow of the Council on Foreign Relations, and a founding member of the Trilateral Commission. As his friend and former mentor Richard Neustadt remarked during the search for Price's successor, Allison was eminently suited for the job, combining "strong scholarship, teaching, and managerial effectiveness."[41]

President Bok announced his appointment of the new dean at the March 1977 meeting of the School's

Dean Don K. Price (LLD '70 hon.) and
Dean Graham T. Allison, Jr. (AB '62,
Ph.D. '68).

Visiting Committee. This concluded a lengthy discussion between Bok, Allison, and John Dunlop, the former dean of the Faculty of Arts and Sciences, about the deanship. Bok first offered the job to Allison almost a year earlier in 1976. But Allison resisted on four grounds: his feeling that he was too young; his hope to go to Washington to gain direct experience in government; his judgment that what the School needed most at this stage was a dean with a capacity to raise funds; and his worry that the School had not yet found a viable conception of its mission and strategy.

That the School's financial problems were serious and urgent, no one disagreed. The savings and foundation grants Price had used to finance the new Public Policy Program had been exhausted. From 1974 to 1977, the School's spending exceeded its income annually by more than $200,000. Harvard's most sacred financial principle decrees: "Every tub on its own bottom." Each school at Harvard is financially independent, responsible for raising and spending its own funds, as long as it remains solvent. The School's deficit had attracted the attention of the University's financial office. The School would either have to cut back immediately or raise new funds. Neither option seemed promising.

Bok and Price had launched a fundraising campaign for Public Policy and Administration after the President's Annual Report in 1974. But the campaign had not succeeded. Toward its $21 million goal, three years later only $1 million had been raised. The School had no wealthy alumni to whom it could turn. Many individuals with capital had an antipathy for government. As Bok and Price found in trying to make the case for the School, the mood in the country reflected more concern about the growing burden of big government than commitment to competence in government. As one person asked at the conclusion of a fundraising pitch for the School: "Why should I give my money to make government smarter at exploiting me better?"

Though less tangible, Allison believed that even more important than money was the need for a coherent mission and strategy. Among his favorite quotations was Nietzsche's observation that "the most common form of human stupidity is forgetting what one is trying to do." The first question he brought to most situations was: What are we trying to do?

The answer for the School remained uncertain. Unquestionably, ambitions were stirring in Harvard's breast. But for what, precisely, no one knew. Nowhere in the United States, or anywhere else, did there exist a model Harvard could emulate.

President Bok's Annual Report of 1973–74 had called for a "new profession" of public service. That report featured four faculties as roughly equal contributors—the School of Government being one, alongside the schools of Design, Education, and Public Health. This concept had a certain plausibility, especially in light of the fact that the School of Government was much the smallest of Harvard's small professional schools. But the concept lacked focus. It had proven difficult to communicate within the University or beyond. For the School of Government, it did little to excite

First commencement at the "new" Kennedy School, June 1979.

Kennedy School faculty members enjoying commencement. In the front row from left: Edith Stokey, Francis Bator, Gerry Mechling, Ronald Heifetz, Robert Reich, Michael O'Hare, Dorothy Robyn; at the end of the second row: Ronald Ferguson.

enthusiasm. From discussions among Bok, Dunlop, and Allison about challenges to the School a consensus emerged about the need for a clearer vision of the enterprise.

At the Visiting Committee meeting where his appointment was announced, Allison unveiled a new vision of the School. He began by recalling the British historian Lord Acton's image of the "remote and ideal objective" that captivates the imagination by its splendor and simplicity and thereby evokes an effort that could not be commanded by lesser and more proximate goals. For the John F. Kennedy School of Government that objective should be "to become a substantial professional school that addresses society's demand for excellence in government in many of the ways Harvard's Schools of Business, Law, and Medicine address analogous demands in their respective private professions."[42]

Given the state of the School in 1977, this objective suitably met Acton's test of remoteness. The core faculty numbered but a dozen; the student body just 200, for only half of whom the faculty offered special courses. By most measures—stu-

At a dinner for the Visiting Committee from left: Shirley Brooks, Frank Weil, Peter Malkin, Stephen Stamas, Nancy Huntington, Harry Kahn, Senator Edward M. Kennedy, Elas Porter, Richard Neustadt.

dents, faculty, budget, and activity—the School stood last among Harvard's nine professional schools.

By making Harvard's schools of Business, Law, and Medicine the relevant analogs for the School of Government, the new objective raised everyone's sights—focusing the mind, without providing a blueprint. Each is a national, even international, leader in building knowledge and training individuals for its respective profession. Each, however, differs significantly from the others, for example, in emphasis on research, size of graduate programs, and role of executive programs. On the one hand, this mission statement directed the School's attention to its professional mission, making the impact of its graduates an inescapable measure of the School's performance. On the other hand, an ambition to serve demands for excellence in a sector that represented a third of the GNP in the United States would require an enterprise of scope and weight. If the School could emulate Harvard's major professional schools in training leadership and building knowledge, it should command the support of

everyone with a stake in public problem-solving.

While setting the sights high, this objective also underlined the extent to which this new venture was of necessity experimental and exploratory. It followed in a time-honored Harvard tradition in establishing a School of Medicine in the eighteenth century, a School of Law in the nineteenth century, and a School of Business at the beginning of the twentieth century. But a School of Government would have to be something else, and more, and different as well.

The strategy Allison developed for the first stage of the effort was organized into three divisions of activity: graduate degree programs, executive programs, and research centers. The most recent version of his chart, reproduced as Figure 1,

reflects the growth of the School over the past nine years. The original chart was quite different. The graduate degree programs included the Public Administration Program as well as the Public Policy Program—a not so subtle reminder to the faculty and others that the School would have to take responsibility for all of its students. Within the box labeled executive programs, there were in 1977 but two, the Institute of Politics' Seminar for Newly Elected Members of Congress, which had enrolled only ten participants, and a Senior Managers in Government Program initiated a year earlier, under the control of the Business School. The new dean was indebted to his colleague Laurence Fouraker, dean of the Business School, for the strategic idea that executive programs should play a cen-

Figure 1

MISSION
Excellence in Government
Excellence in Public Problemsolving

CANONICAL OBJECTIVES
as stated by President Bok

- To be a professional school of government that serves society's demand for excellence in government in many of the ways Harvard's schools of Business, Law, and Medicine serve analogous demands in their respective private professions
- To be the hub of the university-wide program in Public Policy and Management

GRADUATE DEGREE PROGRAMS

- Master in Public Administration (Mid-Career) (244)
- Master in Public Policy (304) (including City and Regional Planning)
- Master in Public Administration (Two Year) (97)
- Ph.D. Programs (33)

TOTAL: 678 Students

EXECUTIVE PROGRAMS

- New Mayors (21)
- New Congressmen (45)
- Massachusetts Executives (40)
- Senior Managers in Government (111)
- National and International Security Managers (94)
- State and Local Executives (118)
- Senior Executive Fellows (40)
- Senior Officials in National Security (65)
- Defense Policy Seminars (40)
- Subcabinet Seminars (80)   TOTAL: 654

RESEARCH CENTERS

- Center for Science and International Affairs
- Energy and Environmental Policy Center
- Center for Business and Government (including Regulation and Capital Formation)
- Center for Health Policy and Management
- Center for Criminal Justice Policy and Management
- Institute of Politics (including Public Affairs Forum)
- State, Local, and Intergovernmental Center (including Joint Center for Housing Studies)
- Joan Shorenstein Barone Center on Press, Politics, and Public Policy

- Harvard Institute for International Development

Laurence Lynn, Jr. (AM '74 hon.), professor of public policy and chairman of the Public Policy Program from 1978 to 1983, teaching a group of senior managers in government.

tral role in shaping the School's self-concept. Nothing so wonderfully concentrated faculty members' minds on professional problems facing managers in government as the necessity to stand up before them in a classroom.

The third division of activity on the chart is research centers, although in 1977 this box contained only the Institute of Politics. The Institute had earlier sponsored some research, but it had been sacrificed in favor of the IOP's Fellows program and activities for undergraduates, while the Institute's resources had been committed to developing the Public Policy Program. Research centers would be important not only in providing ideas for the School's teaching programs, but also in clarifying major issues of public policy. As the executive programs provided an anchor to the profession, research centers provided an anchor to complex public policy issues, guarding against the risk that the faculty might become too abstractly methodological. According to the strategy, faculty members were not members of departments or attached to any divisions, but participated in

the activity of all three components of the School. This tri-partite strategy offered for the first time a conception of a comprehensive school of government committed to training individuals for career, appointed, and elected positions; for addressing issues at the city, state, national, and international levels; and for seeking solutions to public policy problems—thinking not only about government, but also about interactions between government and private sectors in public problem-solving.

Allison's original statement of mission and strategy focused the attention of the School. His three divisions of activity thus provide suitable headings for this chapter's discussion of the School's emergence. But first, attention must be given to a related strand that played

a subtle, but quite deliberate role in shaping the School's conception of what it was about.

The New Littauer Center of Public Administration

The dedication of the new Littauer Center of Public Administration in the fall of 1978 was, in effect, a debut. The 100,000 square foot building gave physical expression to the ambitions of a substantial professional school. Previously, the School had squeezed into one corner of the old Littauer Center (of which it was the nominal owner). The Institute of Politics was located across campus in a little yellow house that offered no room for expansion. The new site

The "new" School of Government. This building reflects Harvard's past and its future, with modern counterparts of Harvard brick chimneys, slate roofs, and gabled ends of buildings.

Opposite; right: Maestro Arthur Fiedler conducts the Harvard Band at the 1978 dedication.

on the river, just across from the Business School and adjacent to the undergraduate College, provided space for the School to spread its wings.

The dedication ceremonies were festive, solemn, and stirring. Among those present for the occasion were the Kennedy clan (Teddy, Jacqueline Onassis, the sisters, and the children) and veterans of the new frontier (McGeorge Bundy and Arthur Schlesinger, Jr., among others). Arthur Fiedler led the Harvard Band. An unscheduled protest added to the excitement, if not the order, of the occasion. An audience numbering more than 10,000 witnessed the event. This entire "production" was directed by a woman drafted out of retirement three months before the dedication. Her energy, imagination, standards, and taste quickly made her an institution at the Kennedy School. Known as "Johnny" to her colleagues and friends, Elizabeth Fainsod was one of those few people whose work came to define the School.

The design and construction of the new building suggested clues to the new dean's management style.

First, the building said "Harvard." It explicitly harkened back to Harvard traditions. In contrast to the concrete faces of other recent Harvard construction, like the Holyoke Center or the School of Design, the Kennedy School's facade is the brick of Harvard Yard. The absence of concrete or steel on the School's facade was no accident. The architect's first design had been all concrete and glass; the second design half concrete. It was argued that clothing the exterior in brick would be disingenuous, since this disguised rather than disclosed the structural integrity of the building. But the new dean disagreed—and had his way.

In walks around Harvard yard with the architects, Allison repeatedly asked: "What are the distinctive, recurring features of build-ings constructed over three centuries?" In addition to brick, these "tours" identified several further elements: chimneys, slate roofs, and gabled ends of buildings, which an associate named "colonial monitors." The new building included modern counterparts of each.

The name of the new building—the new Littauer Center of Public Administration—symbolized a revival of the School's Littauer tradition. One of Dean Allison's first projects had been to seek a reconciliation with Harry Starr, president of the Littauer Foundation, who had understandably been estranged by Harvard's decision to rename the School in 1966. As part of the dedication ceremonies, Harvard renamed the major program from the earlier period the Littauer Public Administration Program, revived the practice of awarding Littauer Fellowships to the most distinguished participants in the program, and restored a second Littauer professorship in the School (to which Richard E. Neustadt was appointed). Heinrich Bruening, the former German chancellor, had been the first to hold this chair; it had lapsed on his return to Germany after the defeat of Hitler. Speakers at the special Littauer dedication included Harry Starr, Elliot Richardson (chairman of the Visiting Committee), and Leverett Saltonstall (former Senator and member of the School's Visiting Committee).

This deliberate attention to the School's history and to Harvard's tradition of public service sounded a theme that echoes even today. Recollection of Harvard's historic traditions enhanced the legitimacy and

Elizabeth C. Reveal, an alumna of the School (MPA '81), became budget director, District of Columbia, before returning to the School in 1985 as associate dean for administration.

Top left: Elizabeth "Johnny" Fainsod (AM '37), executive assistant to Dean Allison from 1978 to 1986, produced what the *Boston Globe* subsequently labeled "the biggest bash Boston has seen since Isabella Stewart Gardner invited Brahmin society to see her new home on the Fenway."

Top right: The City of Cambridge's decision to change the name of Boylston St. to John F. Kennedy St. elicited some controversy.

stature of the new enterprise. By actively reaching out to Harvard graduates in government and making them part of the new venture, the School gained not only wise counsel but also able constituents.

Another characteristic of Allison's management style was apparent in his selection of a partner to manage the process of design and construction. A former chief of staff to Mayor Ken Gibson in Newark and Mayor Kevin White in Boston, Ira Jackson graduated from the MPA program in 1976. A high-energy, high-morale, highflier with a capacity for inspired concentration, Jackson saw that the building was completed on time and under budget. In the construction management, as in other assignments, Jackson set a high standard of quality for the School's central administrative team, which has been carried on by his successors, Hale Champion, Robert Blackwill, and Betsy Reveal.

A third managerial trait was conservatism with a small c. One of "Allison's Laws" states: There are ninety-nine plausible ways to do something wrong for every one way to do it right. Invoking this repeat-

edly throughout the design process, Allison, Jackson, and the architects spent more time identifying and assessing working examples of what they wanted in the building than in modifying the examples they considered successful. In designing classrooms for case-based teaching, they surveyed similar classrooms at the Law and Business schools and evaluated the advantages of tiered seating, swivel chairs, desk styles, even the location of the clocks (the Law School classrooms having first located clocks on the front wall where they could be seen by the students but not the instructor). In selecting the lighting, the style of offices, and interior design, including colors and textures, the School's management paid consummate attention to detail. Unlike other recent construction at Harvard, new Littauer has windows that can be opened. Harvard's Planning Office opposed this vehemently, arguing variously that it violated fire codes, reduced energy efficiency, and was unnecessary because of modern heating and air conditioning systems. The argument was settled on a sultry summer afternoon in the of-

Ira Jackson (AB '70, MPA '76) then associate dean, managed the construction of the first building, which was completed on time and under budget.

Above right: At the 1978 dedication ceremony: former Governor Leverett Saltonstall, former U.S. House Speaker Carl Albert, and then Boston Mayor Kevin White.

fice of the chief planner in Holyoke Center—where the temperature approached 90 degrees.

A final managerial aspect exhibited in the new building might be labeled targeted boldness. The exterior of the new building was intended to make no dramatic architectural statement. Quite deliberately, the cornice of the new building was slightly lower than those of Eliot and Kirkland Houses across the street. But inside, the new building expressed one bold architectural idea: the Forum.

The notion of a forum emerged in late-night conversations between Jackson and Allison. They wanted a physical expression of the School's raison d'être. Jackson admired the Roman forum. Allison recalled the Greek agora, a focus of conversation, commerce, philosophy, and politics.

Together they visited several New England town meeting halls and assigned a research assistant to construct a cardboard version of what they had in mind. The chairman of the School's Visiting Committee, Frank Stanton, declared the model a "winner," expanded it to include a 5' by 10' television screen, and enlarged the conception of events that could be held in the space. He then presented the proposition to the Atlantic Richfield Corporation, whose president, Thornton Bradshaw, was a fellow member of the School's Visiting Committee. Bradshaw liked it and the ARCO Public Affairs Forum was born.

Others at Harvard remained skeptical about "creating a mausoleum" at the center of the School. Multiple-use space is notoriously tricky. No one could find a successful

Bishop Tutu

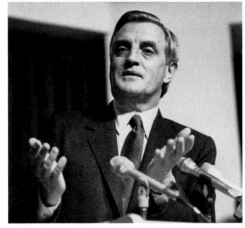

Walter Mondale

Betty Friedan

Art Buchwald

Shirley Williams

McGeorge Bundy

Ben Bradlee

Mario Cuomo

I.F. Stone

Opposite: Speakers communicate with their hands as well as their voices in the Kennedy School's Forum.

Right: An overflow crowd in the ARCO Forum.

working example of this idea. Nonetheless, once Stanton had secured funding from ARCO, the architects transformed the models and dreams into an architectural gem. Balanced in symmetry, elegant in simplicity, the Forum's utility exceeded all expectations. A unique mixture of agora, forum, and town meeting hall, the Forum is abuzz with conversation among students and faculty at all hours. A series of concentric rings function as lounges where students can read a case or just have a cup of coffee. Carpeted risers provide indoor steps on which students can sit and talk year-round. These steps reflect Tom Schelling's observation that as a graduate student, he learned more from his classmates while sitting on the steps of old Littauer than from his classes. Because of inclement weather, this truncated his education during Cambridge's long winters. An indoor cafe at lunchtime and a suitably unstructured, multilayered theater-in-the-round equipped for multimedia presentations and debates in the evening, in the words of one observer, "If the ARCO Public Affairs Forum did not exist, someone would now have to invent it."

Graduate Degree Programs

The Kennedy School had just over 200 registered full-time students in 1976. By 1980–81 it had nearly 700, at which point enrollment stabilized. It became the annual pattern to accept about 150 students into the one-year Master of Public Policy (MPP) program, some 250 into the one-year mid-career Master of Public Administration (MPA) program, and another 50 or so into a two-year MPA program. In addition, 40 to 50 Ph.D. candidates remained in residence.

The School's graduate degree programs prepare individuals for positions of leadership in public problem-solving. Most graduates of these programs will work for most of their lives in government: as career offi-cials, in appointed positions, or as elected leaders. In other stages of their careers they may work in the independent sector—nonprofit organizations, international institutions, and foundations—or increasingly in private sector roles for consulting firms, research organizations, and private businesses involved in public problems. The graduate programs attempt to produce neither specialists nor technicians, but to assist students in preparing themselves to make significant contributions to the solution of public problems.

The two-year program changed considerably in 1980 as a result of the transfer of the City and Regional Planning Program from the School of Design to the Kennedy School. In President Bok's view, the overlap between the City and Regional Plan-ning Program and the Public Policy Program was an unnecessary duplication. Moreover, as the CRP program had evolved, it had grown distant from the central mission of the Design School. Rather than maintaining a public policy–style program focused exclusively on cities in one faculty, and a program that trained students for all levels of government in another, Bok concluded that the two should merge within the Kennedy School. Initially, the merger enjoyed little support from either faculty and hot debate ensued. In the end, an agreement was negotiated. Some members of the Design faculty transferred to the Kennedy School. Although there were still to be two separate degrees (a Master of Public Policy and a Master of City and Regional Planning), there could be a single curriculum with a common first-year core and some overlapping elective courses in the second year.

The one-year MPA program, formally the Lucius N. Littauer Public Administration Program, also expanded from its previous number of about 100. Students enrolled in the program continued to have an aver-

age of ten years' experience in government. As the class grew to 250, some 50 were Mason Fellows from developing countries. Most of the other 200 were Americans from the federal government (including the military services, CIA, State Department, and domestic agencies), state governments, local governments, and the independent sector.

A new degree program, the two-year MPA, emerged to meet the needs of students who required more flexibility than the MPP/MCRP curriculum permitted but lacked the experience to qualify for the mid-career MPA. In 1983 the Volkswagen Foundation made a $2 million grant to initiate the McCloy Scholars Program. Named in honor of former U.S. High Commissioner to Germany John J. McCloy, the program brings to the School each year

from the Federal Republic of Germany up to ten students of outstanding academic ability and high leadership potential. Since many of the McCloy Scholars already had or were pursuing professional or higher degrees at home, the MPP/MCRP curriculum was inappropriate for them. The two-year MPA program, however, allowed them to take courses that suited their individual interests. Fashioned after the Rhodes Scholarships, the program's purpose was "to train the scholars in American methods of public management and policy analysis, to acquaint them with alternate visions of human welfare and global issues, and to promote ties between the two countries."[43]

Another of Allison's initiatives was the establishment of the APPAM Summer Minority Program. Spon-

Professor of Public Policy Mary Jo Bane (MAT '66, Ed.D. '72) was the first woman to be appointed full professor in the School.

Above left: The Kennedy School staff, as Dean Allison has said, "is the backbone of the enterprise." Shown here are some recent and long-term staff members. Front row: Erica Hernandez, Martha Kreckler, Jane Carlson, Raine Figueroa, Anne Stamas, Sharyn Imonti, Novella Wooten, Sally Makacynas. Middle row: Penny Corbett, Diane LeBlanc, Yvette Lewis, Mary Naus, Marcia Gonsalves, Claire Boulanger, Bill Neckyfarow. Last row: Polycarpe Gabriel, Roger Joujoute, Jack Hills, Sharon Gale, Bayley Mason, Lupe Caro, Brian Robin, Brian Knapp, Connie Gates, Liza Womack, Bill O'Neil, Patty Walsh, Marianne Stevenson.

McCloy Scholar Rose Gerrit Huy (MPA '85) with McCloy program adviser Henry Kissinger (AB '50, AM '52, Ph.D. '54), John McCloy (LLB '21, LLD '51), and Dean Allison (AB '62, Ph.D. '68) at a New York dinner celebrating McCloy's ninetieth birthday.

sored by the Association for Public Policy Analysis and Management and funded by the Sloan Foundation, it began in 1981 as part of a larger effort to increase minority participation in the upper levels of public service. Its immediate objective was to help minority students strengthen the basic skills they would need to compete effectively in graduate public policy programs to which they had already been admitted. Of the forty or so students usually participating in the program, roughly 25 percent go on to enroll in the Kennedy School the following fall, and the rest enroll in other public policy programs around the country.

Equally important for the School's aspirations was its doctoral program.

From this program would come scholars who would enlarge theoretical understanding of public policy and public management. From it also would come teachers for the new profession.

In the mid-1980s, fifteen years after creation of the degree, there were forty-two Ph.D.s in Public Policy. No fewer than eleven were members of Harvard faculties or fellows at Harvard research centers. Among these were Jose A. Gomez-Ibanez, Robert Klitgaard, Mark Moore, Albert ("Nick") Nichols, and Gregory Treverton of the Kennedy School faculty and Harvey Fineberg, dean of the School of Public Health. Another dozen were faculty members at branches of the University of

California, Carnegie–Mellon, Duke, M.I.T., and other such institutions. Outside the United States, one was at York University in Canada, another at the University of Oslo. Not surprisingly, given the nature of the program, some graduates held research posts at the Environmental Protection Agency, the Federal Trade Commission, the World Bank, or with congressional committees, and others held comparable posts in organizations such as the Cleveland Foundation, Common Cause, the National Conference of State Legislatures, and the Urban Institute.

While the new program was gathering force, the older doctoral program in Political Economy and Government during the same period produced two dozen Ph.D.s, some of whom went on to faculty posts not only at American universities but at institutions in France, Greece, India, and Japan. One, Carlos Salinas de Gortari, is currently a cabinet member in Mexico. Under Francis Bator, then David Wise, then Howard Raiffa, and most recently Ernest May and Nick Nichols, the School's doctoral committee has been steadily laying up intellectual capital for the future benefit of the School and other comparable institutions.

The most distinctive feature of the Public Policy Program, including its MCRP option, continued to be its core curriculum. This was designed less to impart a body of specific knowledge than to develop a way of thinking of public policy problems. The objective common to core courses was to equip students to approach problems with an organized set of questions and a sense of how to go about answering these questions using available evidence and analysis. Students were expected to learn analytic skills in order to become sophisticated consumers of the best analyses of public policy problems.

The faculty's commitment to the core curriculum and its continuous improvement is virtually unprecedented. Of the four original core courses, three had emphasized methodologies grounded in quantitative reasoning. This reflected the then less developed state of political analysis. In time, however, the political analysis course developed by Neustadt, Allison, and Moore became more important and com-

manded a larger portion of students' time. The curriculum review committee Allison chaired just prior to becoming dean concluded that the political analysis course should expand to two courses, one on political organizational analysis and on public management. Professor Mark Moore led a sustained effort to identify teachable and researchable elements of public management.

The one-year MPA program never had a distinctive curriculum. Students designed their own individual programs from course offerings in Arts and Science departments and other professional schools. Little attempt had been made to develop courses specifically tailored to the interests and needs of mid-career students. In the late 1970s, when Professor Thomas Schelling became chairman of the MPA program, he persuaded the Kennedy School faculty to take responsibility for offering such courses. Today, as a result, while students still have the opportunity to take any of several thousand courses in Harvard's various catalogues, they in fact choose two-thirds of their coursework from Kennedy School courses specifically

designed for professional students in government.

In teaching the economics segment of the core curriculum, Thomas Schelling was soon joined by Francis Bator. Richard Zeckhauser, one of the juniors who helped design the original core curriculum, became a professor in the School and head of its research committee. Among the additional faculty were John R. Meyer, the James W. Harpel Professor of Capital Formation and Economic Growth (and, in addition, a former vice chairman of the Union Pacific Corporation); David A. Wise, the John F. Stambaugh Professor of Political Economy; Glenn C. Loury, a professor serving jointly in the School and the Arts and Sciences Afro-American Studies Program; Edith Stokey, who also served as secretary of the faculty; David Ellwood, a labor economist; Herman ("Dutch") Leonard, a specialist in public finance; and, after his return from the Environmental Protection Agency, Albert ("Nick") Nichols.

Howard Raiffa continued to teach decision theory and bargaining theory, but he no longer did so

Above left: Edith Stokey (AB '44, AM '47), lecturer in public policy and secretary of the School since 1974.

Above right: President Derek Bok produces his first spreadsheet for Professor Mary O'Keeffe (AM '79, Ph.D. '81) in the School's new PC lab. The president's annual report for 1985 focused on computers and the University.

Left: Associate Professor Helen "Sunny" Ladd (AM '71, Ph.D. '74) and Professor Herman "Dutch" Leonard (AB '74, AM '76, Ph.D. '79), the School's resident experts on infrastructure.

Right: Mark Moore (MPP '71, Ph.D. '74), Daniel and Florence Guggenheim Professor of Criminal Justice Policy and Management, notes similarity between public management and walking a tightrope.

alone. Among his colleagues were William Hogan, an energy specialist who chaired the Public Policy Program; James Sebenius, an economist with several years' experience in the complex law of the seas negotiations; Mary O'Keeffe; and Shanta Deverajan. Others teaching varieties of empirical analysis included Richard Light, a statistician who was also a professor in the School of Education, and Helen Ladd and Howard S. Bloom, who had come to the School with the MPP/MCRP merger. While Frederick Mosteller continued to teach statistics to Kennedy School students, he left the core courses to others.

After the bifurcation of the original political analysis course, Steven Kelman took the lead in teaching political and organizational analysis, while Mark Moore and Roger Porter shaped a new course on public management. A prolific writer on incentive systems in the medical profession and in relation to health, safety, and environmental regulation, Kelman had also served with the Federal Trade Commission. The Daniel and Florence Guggenheim Professor of Criminal Justice Policy and Man-

agement, Moore had worked in the Justice Department's Drug Enforcement Administration and was author of several analytical works on the regulation of drug and alcohol abuse. Porter, who served on the White House Staff in both the Ford and Reagan administrations, has written chiefly on the making of foreign economic policy.

Backing Kelman, Moore, and Porter in their innovative teaching efforts were, among others, Mary Jo Bane, a former deputy assistant secretary in the Department of Education and specialist on poverty and policies affecting families; Walter Broadnax, a specialist on human resources policies and formerly a principal deputy assistant secretary in Health and Human Services; Robert Leone, a former member of the Harvard Business School faculty and former senior economist for the President's Council of Economic Advisers; Nancy Altman Lupu, a lawyer with Washington experience both on Capitol Hill and in the Department of Education; Michael O'Hare, an engineer and architect, previously assistant secretary for policy in the Massachusetts

Executive Office of Environmental Affairs; Gary Orren, an expert on polling and a self-styled "political junkie"; Robert Reich, author of best-selling books on American industrial policy; and James Verdier, a lawyer with eight years' experience in the Tax Analysis Division of the Congressional Budget Office.

To supplement the core, the School's faculty offered a panoply of electives, some dealing with analytic methodologies, others with substantive areas of public policy. A random selection of course titles hints at their variety: Economics of Managerial Decisions, by Professor John Meyer; Empirical Analysis for Public Choice, by Professor David Wise; Uses of History for Analysis and Management, by professors May and Neustadt; The Management of Politics, by Professor Gary Orren; Ethics and Public Policy, by Professor William Kristol; and Research Seminar in Leadership, by Dr. Ronald Heifetz (an M.D., psychiatrist, and Juilliard-trained cellist). Beyond the list of methods courses, a much larger number appear under the rubrics of Energy and Environmental Policy, Human Resources,

The School's faculty combines scholarship and practical experience. Seen here (clockwise from left): Professor Richard E. Neustadt, former presidential adviser and expert on the presidency; Richard Darman, former lecturer in public policy, currently assistant to President Reagan; Executive Dean Hale Champion, former undersecretary of health, education, and welfare; Professor Roger Porter, former deputy assistant to the president for policy development and director of the White House Office of Policy Develop-

Health Policy, International Affairs and Security, Transportation, Government and Business, Criminal Justice, Science and Technology, International Development, Urban Economic Development, or Housing and Community Development. Kennedy School course offerings became as distinctive, and as practitioner oriented, as those of any other Harvard professional school.

Executive Programs

Modeled after the Business School's advanced management programs for senior businessmen, executive programs were among the School's most distinctive growth sectors during Allison's deanship. The Institute of Politics had pioneered by inaugurating one-week programs first for newly elected members of Congress, then for newly elected mayors. Allison envisioned programs that would attract other elected and appointed officials, career government servants too senior for the mid-career program, and also members of private sector organizations. Material from courses developed for the School's master's programs provided a starting point, but a cardinal goal was to produce feedback between curricula in the executive and master's programs.

Initially, the core faculty expected to develop executive programs as a junior partner of the Business School. The early venture, the Program for Senior Managers in Government, was organized to run for three weeks each summer and designed for upper-level federal civic servants and representatives of the private sector. Joseph Bower from the Business School presided and the faculty was mixed. Though participants found the program exciting and believed they learned a great deal, many commented that the segments taught by Business School and Kennedy School faculty seemed sharply and qualitatively different. The faculty members themselves increasingly came to doubt the efficacy of mixing approaches. While the Business School approach emphasized management technique regardless of context, that of the Kennedy School accentuated the specifics of particular policy areas or particular bureaucracies. Moreover, differences in emphasis between public and private management were becoming clearer to both faculties.

In the meantime the School had launched a second executive program for National and International Security Managers. It was designed primarily for flag and general officers of the military services and for civilians of comparable level from the State and Defense departments, the intelligence community, and congressional committee staffs.

ment; and Professor Joseph Nye, former deputy to the undersecretary of state for security assistance, science, and technology, and an expert on nuclear proliferation.

Some of the Kennedy School's lighter traditions: volleyball, the talent show, and jogging along the Charles River.

Right: At the talent show: Lecturer in Public Policy Robert Reich performs as the "Albanian Prime Minister" while Associate Professor of Public Policy Michael Nacht serves as his interpreter.

Below left: . . . and about to score a point, Albert "Nick" Nichols, now associate professor of public policy, faces Associate Professor of Public Policy Robert Klitgaard.

Below right: Gregory Treverton, lecturer in public policy; H. James Brown, professor of city and regional planning and director of the State, Local, and Intergovernmental Center; Martin Linsky, lecturer in public policy; and Walter Broadnax, lecturer in public policy.

Allison and May had dreamed up the idea while en route to a tennis weekend in New Hampshire. They took their proposal to the Business School but found little interest there in a second collaborative venture. Hugo Uyterhoven, one of the Business School's star teachers, agreed to take part; otherwise, the Kennedy School was left on its own. Allison and May went ahead with a two-week program. It proved an unqualified success and has remained so.

Thereafter, under Assistant Dean Pete Zimmerman, executive programs grew to become a major feature of the School. Together with the School's Executive Dean, former Under Secretary of Health, Education, and Welfare (and former IOP Fellow) Hale Champion giving the program general oversight and Nancy Arkelyan Huntington providing day-to-day management, the School assumed primary responsibility for the Senior Managers in Government Program. It, too, was an unqualified success. A thirteen-week program for Senior Executive Fellows began in 1979. Its target audience was the federal Senior Executive Service and managers of comparable rank in state and local government and the private sector. There followed a three-week summer program for Senior Executives in State and Local Government, chaired in recent years by Marc J. Roberts, an economist, a professor in both the Kennedy School and the School of Public Health, and author of various works on public sector and private sector choicemaking. Under a contract with the Department of Defense, the School developed an eight-week executive program for Senior Offi-cials in National Security, which enrolled military officers at the rank of colonel and Navy captain and civilian officials of comparable rank. This program soon grew to include participants from the State Department and the Central Intelligence Agency. Former Under Secretary of the Navy Robert Murray (MPA 1967), the School's director of National Security Studies, now manages it and the summer program in National and International Security.

Apart from executive programs that became regular offerings, the School also developed programs for special audiences. After 1981, under a unique arrangement with the White House, the School's faculty offered short seminars on the development of strategy and management techniques for senior presidential appointees at the assistant secretary level. A product of discussions between IOP Director Jonathan Moore and Presidential Counselor Edwin Meese, the program focused on case studies involving specific problems of past and current appointees. Modeled along these same lines was a program providing one-week training sessions for top executives of the

Commonwealth of Massachusetts in such areas as human resource management, financial management and control, and operations management.

Research Centers

The third division for development during Allison's deanship was applied research programs organized in specialized research centers. Each center was to examine a set of major contemporary public policy issues. The goal was a more integrated, interdisciplinary, and inter-faculty approach to research than had been possible in previous patterns.

As with executive programs, so with interdisciplinary and inter-faculty research, the Institute of Poli-

tics had explored the terrain. As described in Chapter 3, Neustadt inspired formation of the "May group." This acquired in time a more formal existence and a ponderous title, the IOP Research Seminar on Bureaucracy, Politics, and Public Policy. Its membership broadened and divided into subgroups. Eventually, it left the IOP to become the Kennedy School Case Program, generating materials to be used in new courses and executive programs.

Under May, Neustadt's immediate successor as director, and under Jonathan Moore, director since 1974, the IOP continued to promote study that entailed direct interaction between professors and practitioners. Every four years, beginning in 1972, it sponsors a conference in which academics and journalists analyze election tactics, mistakes, and successes with managers of the just-concluded U.S. presidential campaign. The IOP director then edits the proceedings into a book. Continuing a practice originated by Neustadt, the IOP also regularly conducts an unpublicized, independent inquiry into problems likely to arise in the transition period if a new

president were to be elected. After the election, whenever an actual transition occurred, the IOP director provides the results to the newly elected president's transition team. Aides to presidents Nixon, Carter, and Reagan have testified that they found the documents useful. Indeed, President Nixon cited Henry Kissinger's partial authorship of the 1968 transition study as one of the reasons for Kissinger's selection as National Security Assistant.[44] With grants from the Ford Foundation and the Sloan Foundation, the IOP commissioned in 1983 an analytical history of recent presidential transitions, to be published around the time of the School's semicentennial.[45]

Moore, the first practitioner to be the IOP director, returned to the School (he had received an MPA in

Paul M. Doty (AM '50 hon.), Mallinckrodt Professor of Biochemistry and director emeritus of the Center for Science and International Affairs.

1957 and was an IOP fellow in 1966–67), having added experience in national presidential campaigns and as counselor at the Department of Health, Education, and Welfare and associate U.S. attorney general to his foreign policy experience. He greatly increased the number of conferences, workshops, and other events that drew undergraduates to the School and brought various Harvard communities into touch with representatives from the world of government and politics not otherwise represented in Cambridge—particularly elected officials, people concerned with campaigns and elections, and political journalists. The IOP also developed special television documentaries and public affairs programs and took the lead in developing a new center for the study of relations between the media and government.

After the IOP, the next of the School's research centers was the Center for Science and International Affairs (CSIA). Originally organized in 1973 as the Program for Science and International Affairs, it became part of the Kennedy School in 1978 as part of a $4 million grant from

the Ford Foundation. Under its former director, Paul Doty, and his successor, Joseph Nye, the Center's research focuses on international security affairs, with a special emphasis on the impact of science and technology. Doty, a professor of biochemistry, had long been a leader in efforts to develop workable arms control formulas. Nye, a professor of government, was deputy to the under secretary of state in the Carter Administration and chair of the NSC committee that developed policies to limit proliferation of nuclear weapons. Throughout its years under both Doty and Nye, the Center's seminars and special projects were managed by Dr. Dorothy Shore Zinberg. Albert Carnesale, a nuclear engineer with experience in Washington and a professor of public policy in the Kennedy School, was associate director of CSIA before becoming academic dean of the School. He remains one of its senior research associates. Dr. Stephen J. Flanagan, formerly on the staff of the Senate Select Intelligence Committee, became executive director, and physicist and former Rhodes Scholar Ashton Carter, after joining

the School, became the Center's assistant director.

The Center plays host each year to approximately ten postdoctoral and mid-career research fellows and an equal number of doctoral degree candidates from Harvard and elsewhere. It also has some longer-term research associates, among them (in addition to Carnesale) William W. Kaufmann, a leading authority on defense budgets. The Center conducts a broad array of conferences; maintains a small, specialized library in international affairs; and sponsors and edits *International Security*, one of the leading journals in its field.

In the mid-1980s the CSIA undertook several new projects. The Project on Avoiding Nuclear War was an interdisciplinary study supported by a grant from the Carnegie Corpora-

Coauthors of *Hawks, Doves, and Owls: An Agenda for Avoiding Nuclear War:* Dean Graham Allison, Jr. (AB '62, Ph.D. '68), Academic Dean Albert Carnesale (AM '78 hon.), and CSIA Director Joseph Nye (Ph.D. '64), principal coinvestigators of the School's Project on Avoiding Nuclear War.

tion. Directed jointly by Allison, Carnesale, and Nye, the project's primary aim was to explore and suggest realistic ways of reducing the likelihood of a major nuclear war. Some of its findings were summarized in its first major publication, *Hawks, Doves, and Owls: An Agenda for Avoiding Nuclear War* (1985) by Allison, Carnesale, and Nye. Its second major product was *Nuclear Ethics* (1986) written by Nye. Related projects currently underway include Explicating the Arms Control Debate, a study sponsored by the Rockefeller Brothers and W. Alton Jones Foundations that seeks to resolve disputes that divide national policy on arms control, and Learning from Experience with Arms Control, a study funded by the U.S. Arms Control and Disarmament Agency to explore the lessons that

may be learned from past U.S.-Soviet arms control accords.

The School added four more research centers, and it is now creating yet another. One newcomer was the Energy and Environmental Policy Center. It was formed in 1979 and has been headed continuously by Professor William Hogan, with Henry Lee as executive director. Hogan is a former official of the Federal Energy Administration, and Lee directed the Energy Office of the Commonwealth of Massachusetts from 1970 to 1979. The Center draws faculty and student researchers with interest in energy problems, foreign affairs, and economics from schools and departments across the University. In addition to such concerns as the development, regulation, and conservation of energy, the Center analyzes such subjects as

long-term relationships between energy and national and international security. While there are several energy research centers in the United States, few have a comparably active environmental policy component. One member of the School's core faculty active in the Energy Center as well as in CSIA is Harvey Brooks, the Benjamin Peirce Professor of Technology and Public Policy, longtime head of the Division of Engineering and Applied Physics in the Faculty of Arts and Sciences, and a noted influence in national science policies.

The Center for Health Policy and Management is currently directed by Dr. David Blumenthal. Both a physician and a graduate of the school's Public Policy Program, Dr. Blumenthal served in Washington on the staff of the Senate Subcommittee on Health and Scientific Research chaired by Senator Edward M. Kennedy. The original concept developed out of discussions in the late 1970s involving Allison, Bok, Dunlop, and Dean Robert Ebert of the Medical School. Founded in 1980 with Dr. David Hamburg as director, the Center functions as part of the

Left: Harvey Brooks (Ph.D. '40, JD '63 hon.), Benjamin Peirce Professor of Technology and Public Policy, professor of applied physics, and former dean of the Division of Applied Sciences.

Right: Professor William W. Hogan, director of the Energy and Environmental Policy Center and chairman of the School's Public Policy Program.

university-wide Division of Health Policy Research and Education. As such, it is an institutional link between the Kennedy School and the Medical School and the School of Public Health. Along with its research activities, the Center sponsors a Health Policy Seminar Series and a Mental Health Policy Forum and offers courses at the School in health policy.

In 1980–83, when Dr. Hamburg was director of the School's Center for Health Policy and Management, he recruited Professor Thomas C. Schelling for a working group on Health Promotion and Disease Prevention. The two developed plans for an integrated study of what made smoking such a hard habit to quit and of public and private policies that might help people to quit. With an estimated 350,000 prema-

ture deaths each year in the United States attributable to smoking, and with individual behavior far more important than medical practice in prevention of such self-massacre, this specific focus on cigarettes appeared amply justified. When Dr. Hamburg left the School to become president of the Carnegie Corporation, the study plans were not abandoned; a grant in 1984 from that Foundation enabled Professor Schelling to establish within the School the Institute for the Study of Smoking Behavior and Policy.

The Center for Business and Government is another program that traces back to the late 1970s. After serving as secretary of labor, John Dunlop returned to his post as Lamont University Professor and organized an examination of relationships between business and government. One result of that effort was *Business and Public Policy* (1980) edited by Dunlop, with contributions by Bok; eminent business historian, Alfred D. Chandler, Jr.; former Secretary of Labor and soon-to-be Secretary of State George P. Schultz; Dupont Chairman Irving S. Shapiro; Richard Darman and Lau-

rence Lynn of the Kennedy School faculty; and Hugo Uyterhoven. The final chapter, written by Dunlop, made a case for the University's hiring new professors and supporting staff so that, from different vantage points, the Business School and the Kennedy School could pursue convergent work on business-government relations. Dunlop wrote:

There is a critical need in the education of both business executives and public administrators, particularly in executive-level programs, for each to understand not merely the substantive issues of these areas of governmental activity and the decision making processes of business and government but also to appreciate the setting, constraints, and personal context in which the opposite number operates.

The present career patterns of business and government executives and administrators warrant review and adjustment in personnel and compensation policies in both careers to facilitate development of more sensitive and perceptive business leaders and more understanding and competent government officials. It would be helpful if more business enterprises could plan to provide a period of time, such as two to four years, for more executives to work in government as a normal part of their development. Similarly, present governmental executives should be encouraged to spend comparable periods in private industry. A greater degree of two-way mobility across the public–private line would in time make a major contribution to dealing with the issues of isolation and parochialism raised earlier. This would require that our present conflict of interest concepts, as they are practiced, be changed significantly. Even within the present framework of attitudes, more could be done to enhance interchange through recruitment policies, particularly in the government.[46]

Exxon, the Ford Motor Company, and IBM contributed $1 million each for the establishment of new professorships for this purpose.

The Center formally came into existence in 1982. With the assistance of then AEtna Chairman John Filer, and the wise counsel of Anne Wexler, a member of the School's Visiting Committee, a former political and presidential adviser, and the chairman of one of Washington's most successful lobbying firms, the AEtna Foundation and the Kennedy School created a pilot program that focused on the new Center's mission: the Public Policy and Corporate Management Program. Its aim was to recognize senior corporate management as part of both the problem and the solution to public problems, and to encourage a more effective collaboration between business and government. A $1.25 million grant from the AEtna Foundation created both this program and a professorship in the new Center.

A generous gift from Frank Weil, a distinguished Washington lawyer and a member of the School's Visiting Committee, established "Weil Hall," which would house the Business and Government Center in a second building of the School. This new building was constructed with a major gift from Robert Belfer, a

1958 alumnus of the Law School, member of the School's Visiting Committee, and president of Belco Petroleum. The "Robert and Renee Belfer Center for Public Management" was dedicated in October 1984 and now houses administrative offices, research centers, and the Center for Business and Government in Weil Hall.

The Business and Government Center is currently headed by Professor Winthrop Knowlton. Once a Baker Scholar at the Harvard Business School, later an assistant secretary of the treasury, and, before coming to the Kennedy School faculty, the chief executive officer of Harper and Row, Knowlton's full title is Henry R. Luce Professor of Ethics, Business, and Public Policy. The Center's research agenda is organized around four principal areas of public-private concern: public-private partnerships at the state and local levels, capital formation and economic growth, reform of the regulatory process, and the overriding problem of American competitiveness in a global economy. Among active associates of the Center, in addition to professors

Meyer, Zeckhauser, Leonard, and Altman Lupu, is Raymond Vernon, the Clarence Dillon Professor of International Affairs, emeritus and founding editor of the *Journal of Policy Analysis and Management.*

The State, Local, and Intergovernmental Center now embodies the School's commitment to research and teaching on major issues at the state and local levels. This emphasis in the School was expanded in the late 1970s when Allison brought to the School former Governor Michael Dukakis as director of state and local programs. A rare combination of political and managerial talent plus intellectual curiosity, Dukakis developed the School's executive program for state and local senior executives and taught courses in state and local management, along with two other distinguished practitioners, Manuel Carballo and Gordon Chase. The current director of this Center is Professor H. James Brown, chairman of the School's City and Regional Planning Program. The Center actively involves many members of the School's core faculty, including professors Meyer, Ladd, and Leonard; Executive Dean

. . . during . . .

Champion; Professor John F. Kain, author of *The Urban Transportation Problem* and *Housing Markets and Racial Discrimination*; and Professor Jose A. Gomez-Ibanez, an authority on transportation policy and economics.

The newest research center is the Joan Shorenstein Barone Center on Press, Politics, and Public Policy, announced in 1986. It will focus on interactions between the media and government. Expanding upon the Institute of Politics' base in research and outreach fostering better reporting about government, the Center is intended to enhance appreciation of the role of the press by public officials and induce greater understanding of the impact of the press on political institutions. The Frank Stanton Professor of the First Amendment will play a major role in the development of this Center.

While the School's many centers and programs have stimulated research, they have neither monopolized nor confined it. Among faculty publications of 1985–86 that originated outside of any of the specialized centers or programs were May's *Knowing One's Enemies: Intelli-*

. . . and after.

Groundbreaking for the Belfer Center for Public Management: Robert A. Belfer (JD '58), Frank Weil (AB '53, MBA '55), Dean Allison (AB '62, Ph.D. '68), Renée Belfer, and Frank Stanton.

Frank Weil (AB '53, JD '56), a member of the Visiting Committee, who made possible the creation of Weil Hall, shares a light moment with Business and Government Center Director Winthrop Knowlton (AB '53, MBA '55), Henry R. Luce Professor of Ethics.

gence Assessment before the Two World Wars; May and Neustadt's *Thinking in Time: The Uses of History for Decisionmakers;* John D. Montgomery's *Aftermath: Tarnished Outcomes of American Foreign Policy;* O'Hare's *Facility Siting and Public Opposition* (with Will Lawrence Bacow and Debra Sanderson); former Dean Price's *America's Unwritten Constitution: Science, Religion, and Political Responsibility;* Sebenius' *Negotiating the Law of the Sea;* Schelling's *Choice and Consequence: Perspectives of an Errant Economist;* and Treverton's *Making the Alliance Work: The United States and Western Europe.*

Indeed, the major item on the School's recent intellectual agenda, public management, has been developed in conjunction with executive program curriculum, assisted by all the centers. This effort begins with a definition of public management as what the most effective public managers know and do that their counterparts do not. Recognizing that public managers face an array of recurring problems, the School's public management research is trying to capture lessons learned. In-

dividually, public managers learn on the job—sometimes about how not to do a particular task, sometimes about how to do it successfully. As a result, they become smarter. But their learning frequently serves primarily to make the individual manager more productive and has only limited benefit to other managers.

The public management research effort has sought to characterize recurring managerial problems, identify successes and failures in dealing with those problems, document best practices, and analyze lessons learned. The case materials developed in this way provide students with vicarious experience, an opportunity to learn from the failures and even the successes of others, as well as their own. This information also provides a body of data from which

the faculty can extract more general lessons.

The School's basic strategy for the development of a field of public management was described by Allison in 1979 to the Public Management Research Conference. Elements of that strategy include:

developing a significant number of cases on public management problems and practices; analyzing cases to identify better and worse practice; promoting systematic comparative research of management positions in a single agency over time and of similar management positions among several public agencies; and linking research to the training of public managers.[47]

In addition, the strategy includes an announced plan to appoint six professors of public management

Manuel Carballo (LLB '66, MPA '67), lecturer in public policy. After Manny's untimely death, the School established the Manuel Carballo Award for Excellence in Teaching, which was given to Jose Gomez-Ibanez in 1984 and to Mary O'Keeffe in 1985.

over a five-year period, putting this development on a fast track within the School; the recruitment and management of key junior faculty in order to give them a chance to compete for these positions; an extensive case program that provides both teaching and research material; and tight linkage between the public management research agenda and the executive teaching programs. The architect and manager of this effort to develop public management has been Professor Mark Moore. It is fitting that the strategy led to the first two appointments as full professor in 1986, Steven J. Kelman and Herman "Dutch" Leonard.

Outreach and Fundraising

The development of all these activities required resources: not only money, but also credible links with markets. To succeed, it was necessary to engage leaders of American society in making the case for the new venture. Allison began with the School's Visiting Committee, the chairman of which was Elliot Rich-

ardson, former Secretary of Defense, Secretary of Health, Education and Welfare, and Attorney General, who had been fired by President Nixon in the "Saturday night massacre." Richardson believed in the idea of the School and was persuasive with many groups. But as a conservative tide began to rise in the country, the School had to reach out to other constituencies as well. One trigger name at the time was John Connally (former governor of Texas who had been wounded in Dallas when President Kennedy was assassinated, and former secretary of the treasury and of defense). Connally visited the School, liked what he saw, and became an advocate. As he argued in a public lecture at Harvard:

I first went to Washington as a young man, twenty-two years old, in 1939. I have watched this government at all levels. I must say the most exciting thing that I've seen in a very long time, if not in my lifetime, is what Harvard proposes to do with their School of Government. . . . Harvard started out in the School of Business to do something new and unusual and untried, and they have had a remarkable success. President Bok, Dean Al-

lison, and others believe that if it can be done in the Business School, it can be done in the John F. Kennedy School of Government.[48]

When Richardson's term was completed, Frank Stanton became the next chairman of the Visiting Committee. President of CBS for a quarter of a century, Stanton was a legend in the world of broadcasting, an architect of the operational meaning of the First Amendment in his generation, and a blue chip captain of industry. That Stanton was a member of Harvard's Overseers, and thus eligible to be chairman of the Visiting Committee, resulted from Andrew Heiskell's efforts to bring more "weight" to the Overseers and its Visiting Committees. A member of the Harvard Corporation, Heiskell

The Hon. Elliot Richardson (AB'41, LLB '44), former chairman of the School's Visiting Committee.

Frank Stanton, former chairman of the Kennedy School's Visiting Committee and member of the Harvard Board of Overseers, chats with Dean Allison on the penthouse roof of the Kennedy School.

had telephoned his friend Stanton and said, "I've nominated you to be an overseer." There followed a period of silence and then an Alfonse-Gaston conversation in which Stanton searched for clues to what Heiskell might be talking about. When it became clear that Heiskell's subject was Harvard, Stanton responded, "But Andrew, I never went to Harvard and have no Harvard connection." Heiskell replied, "Serves them right," and hung up.[49] Stanton was elected the first non-Harvard overseer in modern times and became chairman of the School's Visiting Committee. In close partnership with the dean, he attracted to the Visiting Committee esteemed individuals from government, business, and the independent sector, making the Committee among the most effective in the University.

The School's urgent financial problems had been a prime issue in the deliberations about who should succeed Price. Reflecting on the failure of the initial campaign, Bok, Dunlop, Price, and Allison recognized that the School would not be able to continue its current activity, much less entertain new visions, without

The School kicked off its fiftieth anniversary with a debate in Washington between two Harvard alumni: Secretary of Defense Caspar Weinberger (AB '38, JD '41) and Senator Edward M. Kennedy (AB '54) moderated by President Derek Bok and Dean Graham T. Allison, Jr.

successful fundraising. A number of inventive, if desperate suggestions emerged from discussions about how to address this problem. Neustadt proposed that the School continue for another year or two and then threaten to collapse, forcing the University somehow to find the funds to come to its rescue. Allison suggested that he remain associate dean and that Bok enlist Nelson Rockefeller to be dean. Others suggested that the School's activity simply be scaled back.

As part of the arrangements under which Allison became dean, Bok agreed for the University to offset the "structural deficit" of $200,000 per year for the first several years, while he and the new dean searched for outside funds. In fact, the funds to eliminate this offset were found in the first eighteen months.

The School's success in fundraising is one of its most dramatic. From 1977 to 1980 the new dean raised almost $10 million. In 1980 the Harvard Campaign began. As had been agreed in the negotiations about the deanship, the School was included in the Harvard Campaign. Although it focused on the College,

the Campaign also licensed the four smaller professional schools to raise funds during the period and count gifts toward the Harvard Campaign. When the Campaign concluded at the end of 1984, the School had raised over $20 million, which accounted for two-thirds of the funds raised by the professional schools and more than half of all the corporate gifts to the Campaign. In addition, the School had received non-Campaign–related gifts of over $14 million. Thus, during the first eight years of Allison's deanship, the School had succeeded in raising some $50 million, including funds for a score of professional chairs and for two new buildings. As the School celebrates its 50th anniversary, its endowment and capital plant are valued at well over $100 million.

The recipe for this success con-

sisted of equal portions of hard work and imagination. The new vision for the School was compelling. Gifts to the School could be understood as investments in making a difference in the performance of government. A deliberate strategy was developed for specific major donors, the corporate community, foundations, and even the School's alumni. A subcommittee of the Visiting Committee was established as a Development Committee under Chairman Stanton. A lean staff was organized first under Tom Reardon, and then Associate Dean Bayley Mason. In arguing the case for the School, and making it a University priority, President Bok played a key role. At the center was a determined dean with hustle, verve, and an unwillingness to take no for an answer.

Allison's years as dean will be

remembered as a time when a professional school of government finally emerged. In 1981, after reviewing all the major public policy programs in the country, evaluators for the Ford Foundation concluded: "More than any other program, Harvard has evolved toward becoming a full-fledged professional school for training generalists in public policy."[30] In the following year the School's own Visiting Committee, made up of distinguished, independent outsiders led by Frank Stanton and Stephen Stamas, compared the School with other schools in the University. Their verdict:

[T]he strategy by which the School is attempting to fulfill its mission is appropriate . . . ; the School is succeeding in its commitment to provide a standard of teaching equal to that of the Schools of Law and Business . . . ; the quality and mix of the School's faculty seems to us among its strongest points. The senior leadership of the School is in strong, capable, effective hands. [51]

As it marks its fiftieth anniversary, the Kennedy School has emerged as one of Harvard's major professional schools.

NOTES

PHOTO CREDITS

INDEX

KENNEDY SCHOOL FACULTY, 1936–1986

KENNEDY SCHOOL OFFICERS OF ADMINISTRATION, 1937–1986

NOTES

1. *John F. Kennedy School of Government Bulletin* (Winter/Spring, 1979): 4.
2. Speech given by Governor Michael Dukakis in the Forum of the John F. Kennedy School of Government, Cambridge, Mass., fall 1985.
3. Melvin T. Copeland, *And Mark an Era: The Story of the Harvard Business School* (Boston: Little, Brown, 1958), p. 3.
4. James B. Conant, *My Several Lives: Memoirs of a Social Inventor* (New York: Harper & Row, 1970), p. 412.
5. Harry Starr, luncheon speech on the occasion of the fortieth anniversary of the Littauer Center, Cambridge, Mass., December 10, 1976.
6. Author's interview with Harry Starr, New York, N.Y., September 26, 1985.
7. Letter from Lucius N. Littauer to James B. Conant, November 13, 1935, Administrative Records of the Office of the Dean, Kennedy School of Government, Harvard University Archives, Cambridge, Mass.
8. Letter from James B. Conant to Harold W. Dodds, January 4, 1936, Administrative Records of the Office of the Dean, Kennedy School of Government, Harvard University Archives, Cambridge, Mass.
9. Harold W. Dodds, Leonard D. White, William B. Munro, Harold H. Burbank, Morris B. Lambie, and Wallace B. Donham, "The Report of the Commission," *Harvard Alumni Bulletin* 39, no. 17 (February 5, 1937): 531–36.
10. John H. Williams, "Memorandum to Mr. Conant on the Graduate School of Public Administration," January 8, 1947, p. 6, Administrative Records of the Office of the Dean, Kennedy School of Government, Harvard University Archives, Cambridge, Mass.
11. Douglass Brown, et al., *The Economics of the Recovery Program* (New York: McGraw Hill, 1934).
12. Paul A. Samuelson, "Has Economic Science Improved the System?" speech given at the John F. Kennedy School of Government, Cambridge, Mass., March 15, 1986.
13. John H. Williams, "Memorandum to Mr. Conant," p. 20.
14. John H. Williams, "Dedication of the Littauer Center of Public Administration, Cambridge, Mass., Graduate School of Public Administration," in *Harvard University Graduate School of Public Administration Annual Reports, 1937–38, 1947–48* (Cambridge, Mass.: Harvard University Press), p. 8.
15. "Report of the Visiting Committee of the Graduate School of Public Administration," tentative draft, May 7, 1942, Lucius N. Littauer Foundation Records, New York, N.Y.
16. Minutes of the Faculty Meeting, February 16, 1942, Administrative Records of the Office of the Dean, Graduate School of Public Administration, Harvard University Archives, Cambridge, Mass.
17. Letter from William B. Munro to Lucius N. Littauer, March 9, 1942, Littauer Foundation Records, New York, N.Y.

18. Minutes of the Faculty Meeting, March 21, 1944, Administrative Records of the Office of the Dean, Graduate School of Public Administration, Harvard University Archives, Cambridge, Mass.

19. "Statement of School Policy," in Minutes of the Faculty Meeting, May 23, 1944, Administrative Records of the Office of the Dean, Graduate School of Public Administration, Harvard University Archives, Cambridge, Mass., pp. 1–2.

20. Nancy S. Pyle, "The Edward S. Mason Program in Public Policy and Management in Developing Countries: The First Twenty-Five Years," May 1983. (Photocopy.)

21. John H. Williams, "Memorandum to Mr. Conant," p. 5.

22. James B. Conant, "President's Report," in *Official Register of Harvard University: Report of the President of Harvard College and Reports of Departments, 1951–1952* 51, no. 2 (Cambridge, Mass.: Harvard University Printing Office, 1954), p. 23.

23. Paul M. Herzog, "A Study of the Harvard University Graduate School of Public Administration," January 1957, p. 71. (Unpublished.)

24. Ibid., p. 33.

25. Edward S. Mason, *Dean's Report, Graduate School of Public Administration, 1956–1957* (Cambridge, Mass.: Harvard University Printing Office), p. 3.

26. Minutes of the Faculty Meeting, December 18, 1956, pp. 12–13, Administrative Records of the Office of the Dean, Graduate School of Public Ad-

ministration, Harvard University Archives, Cambridge, Mass.

27. Author's interview with Don K. Price, June 2, 1985, Cambridge, Mass.

28. Don K. Price, *Harvard University Graduate School of Public Administration Dean's Report, 1962–1963* (Cambridge, Mass.: Harvard University Printing Office), pp. 5–6.

29. Don K. Price, *Twenty-sixth Annual Report of the Graduate School of Public Administration, 1962–1963* (Cambridge, Mass.: Harvard University Printing Office, p. 6.

30. Interview by Joseph E. O'Connor with Nathan Pusey, June 21, 1967, John F. Kennedy Oral History Collection, Kennedy Presidential Library, Boston, Mass.

31. Ibid.

32. Don K. Price, memorandum, "Conversation re: Kennedy Library Institute and GSPA," July 21, 1964; Don K. Price, memorandum to Robert F. Kennedy, "Proposed Institute or Center of Politics of the Kennedy Memorial Library and Its Potential Relation to the Graduate School of Public Administration," July 23, 1964. Both memorandums in the personal papers of Don K. Price.

33. Letter from Richard E. Neustadt to Franklin L. Ford, November 4, 1965, in the personal papers of Richard E. Neustadt.

34. Letter from Robert F. Kennedy to President and Fellows of Harvard College, June 23, 1966; letter from Nathan M. Pusey to Robert F. Kennedy, June 27, 1966. Both letters in the Administrative

Records of the Office of the Dean, Kennedy School of Government, Harvard University Archives, Cambridge, Mass.

35. Committee on Curriculum and Faculty Appointments, Minutes of Meeting, November 28, 1967, Administrative Records of the Office of the Dean, Kennedy School of Government, Harvard University Archives, Cambridge, Mass.

36. Don K. Price, memorandum, "Agenda for Faculty Meeting, March 12, 1974," March 26, 1974, Administrative Records of the Office of the Dean, Kennedy School of Government, Harvard University Archives, Cambridge, Mass.

37. Don K. Price, "John Fitzgerald Kennedy School of Government," in the *Official Register of Harvard University: Report of the President of Harvard College and Reports of Departments, 1973–1974* (Cambridge, Mass.: Harvard University Printing Office, 1975), p. 5 and *passim*.

38. Don K. Price, *Thirty-eighth Annual Report of the John F. Kennedy School of Government, 1974–1975* (Cambridge, Mass.: Harvard University Printing Office), p. 2.

39. Graham T. Allison, Jr., "John Fitzgerald Kennedy School of Government," in the *Official Register of Harvard University: Report of the President of Harvard College and Reports of Departments, 1977–1978* (Cambridge, Mass.: Harvard University Printing Office, 1979), p. 428.

40. Stephen D. Krasner, "Are Bureaucracies Important (or Allison Wonderland)," *Foreign Policy*, no. 7 (1972): 159–79.

41. Letter from Richard E. Neustadt to

Derek Bok, February 3, 1976, in the personal papers of Richard E. Neustadt.

42. Derek C. Bok quoted in Graham T. Allison, Jr., "John Fitzgerald Kennedy School of Government," in the *Official Register of Harvard University: Report of the President of Harvard College and Reports of Departments* (Cambridge, Mass.: Harvard University Printing Office, 1979), p. 428.

43. Graham T. Allison, Jr., quoted in 'VW Funds Program to Bring Young German Scholars Here," *Harvard University Gazette*, March 25, 1983, p. 1.

44. Carroll Kilpatrick, "Kissinger Is Named by Nixon," *Washington Post*, December 3, 1968, p. A4.

45. Carl Brauer, *Presidential Transitions from Eisenhower through Reagan: Peril and Opportunity* (New York: Oxford University Press, 1986).

46. John Dunlop, *Business and Public Policy* (Cambridge, Mass.: Harvard University Press, 1980), pp. 105–106.

47. Graham T. Allison, Jr., "Public and Private Management: Are They Fundamentally Alike in All Unimportant Respects?" *Setting Public Management Agendas* (Washington, D.C.: United States Office of Personnel Management, February, 1980).

48. "John Connally Visits Harvard," *John F. Kennedy School of Government Bulletin* 2, no. 1 (Spring 1978): 41.

49. Telephone conversation between Andrew Heiskell and Frank Stanton, June 1977.

50. Peter D. Bell, "Graduate Training Programs in Public Policy Supported by the Ford Foundation," January 1981, pp. 7–8. (Unpublished.)

51. "Report of the Overseers Committee to Visit the Kennedy School of Government," November 18, 1982, p. 13. (Unpublished.)

PHOTO CREDITS

Page 2, Derek Bok photo courtesy of Michael Tweed.

Page 3, Littauer Center of Public Administration photo courtesy of Michael Nagy.

Page 4, John T. Dunlop photo courtesy of Martha Stewart; John Harvard statue photo courtesy of the Harvard University News Office.

Page 5, Franklin D. Roosevelt photo courtesy of the Harvard University Archives.

Page 6, Caspar Weinberger photo courtesy of Martha Stewart; Zbigniew Brzezinski photo courtesy of Christopher Brown; Michael Dukakis and appointees photo courtesy of Martha Stewart.

Page 7, Mason Fellows photo courtesy of Martha Stewart.

Page 8, Belfer Center photo courtesy of Michael Nagy.

Page 9, Books photo courtesy of Martha Stewart.

Page 10, Edward M. Kennedy photo courtesy of Rex Yung; Ed Koch photo courtesy of Martha Stewart; Cesar Chavez photo courtesy of David Beach; Thomas P. "Tip" O'Neill, Jr. photo courtesy of the Harvard University News Office; Elliot Richardson photo courtesy of Martha Stewart.

Page 11, "Nightline" photo courtesy of Martha Stewart; presidential primary debate photo courtesy of Martha Stewart.

Page 12, "Advocates" photo courtesy of Martha Stewart; Jack Kemp photo courtesy of Martha Stewart; Jeanne

Kirkpatrick photo courtesy of Martha Stewart; Christopher Dodd photo courtesy of Martha Stewart.

Page 16, Lucius N. Littauer portrait photo courtesy of the Harvard University Archives.

Page 17, Groundbreaking for Littauer Center photo courtesy of the Harvard University Archives.

Page 18, Derek Bok and Harry Starr photo courtesy of the Harvard University News Office.

Page 20, Founding fathers photo courtesy of the Lucius Littauer Foundation.

Page 21, John H. Williams photo courtesy of the Harvard University Archives.

Page 22, Alvin H. Hansen photo courtesy of the Harvard University Archives.

Page 26, Littauer Center photo courtesy of the Boston Herald; Hemenway Gym photo courtesy of the Boston Herald.

Page 27, Hunt Hall photo courtesy of the Harvard University Archives; Littauer Center photo courtesy of the Boston Herald.

Page 28, Harvard Square photo courtesy of the Boston Herald.

Page 31, John Kenneth Galbraith photo courtesy of Peggy McMahon.

Page 32, Edward S. Mason photo courtesy of the Harvard University Archives.

Page 33, Arthur Smithies photo courtesy of the Harvard University News Office.

Page 34, Arthur A. Maass photo courtesy of the Harvard University News Office.

Page 35, Robert R. Bowie photo courtesy of the Harvard University Archives.

Page 36, Deans and Paul Herzog photo

courtesy of the Harvard University News Office.

Page 37, Gertrude Manley photo courtesy of the Manley family.

Page 38, Pierre E. Trudeau photo courtesy of Martha Stewart.

Page 42, Don K. Price photo courtesy of Martha Stewart.

Page 43, John D. Montgomery photo courtesy of Martha Stewart.

Page 44, John F. Kennedy and Nathan Pusey photo courtesy of George Hoyt; John F. Kennedy and Cardinal Cushing photo courtesy of M.V. Fitzgerald.

Page 45, Archibald Cox photo courtesy of the Harvard University News Office.

Page 46, John F. Kennedy photograph courtesy of the *Boston Herald;* Jacqueline Kennedy, Michael Forrestal, and Robert F. Kennedy photo courtesy of the Harvard University News Office.

Page 47, Doorplate photo courtesy of Frank Hill; Institute of Politics photo courtesy of the Harvard University News Office.

Page 48, October 17, 1966, meeting photo courtesy of the Harvard University News Office.

Page 49, Richard E. Neustadt and Katherine Graham photo courtesy of the Harvard University News Office.

Page 50, Library-museum complex design photos courtesy of I.M. Pei & Partners.

Page 51, Library-museum complex design photo courtesy of I.M. Pei & Partners.

Page 52, "Halls of Ivy" cartoon copyright, 1961, Conrad, for the *Denver Post.*

Reprinted with permission, Los Angeles Times Syndicate.

Page 53, Howard Raiffa photo courtesy of Martha Stewart; Tom Schelling photo courtesy of the Harvard University News Office.

Page 54, Jonathan Moore photo courtesy of Martha Stewart.

Page 55, John Lindsay photo courtesy of Rex C. Yung; Vernon Jordan photo courtesy of Peggy McMahon; Ernest May photo courtesy of Martha Stewart.

Page 56, Richard E. Neustadt photo courtesy of Martha Stewart.

Page 57, Richard Zeckhauser photo courtesy of the Harvard University News Office.

Page 58, Robert J. Murray photo courtesy of Martha Stewart.

Page 59, Henry Cisneros photo courtesy of Martha Stewart.

Page 62, Don K. Price and Graham T. Allison photo courtesy of the Harvard University News Office.

Page 64, First commencement photo courtesy of Fredrik D. Bodin; group photo at commencement courtesy of Martha Stewart.

Page 65, Visiting Committee dinner photo courtesy of Martha Stewart.

Page 67, Laurence Lynn photo courtesy of Martha Stewart.

Page 68, New School of Government photos courtesy of Daisy Agee.

Page 69, New School of Government photo courtesy of Nick Wheeler; Arthur Fiedler photo courtesy of David Beach.

Page 70, Elizabeth "Johnny" Fainsod photo courtesy of Fredrik D. Bodin; City of Cambridge cartoon courtesy of Chris Demarest; Elizabeth C. Reveal photo courtesy of Martha Stewart.

Page 71, Ira Jackson photo courtesy of David Beach; dedication ceremony photo courtesy of Lew Hedberg.

Page 72, Bishop Tutu photo courtesy of Martha Stewart; Walter Mondale photo courtesy of Martha Stewart; Betty Friedan photo courtesy of the Harvard University News Office; Art Buchwald photo courtesy of Richard M. Feldman; Shirley Williams photo courtesy of Martha Stewart; McGeorge Bundy photo courtesy of Martha Stewart; Ben Bradlee photo courtesy of Susan Lapides; Mario Cuomo photo courtesy of Martha Stewart; I.F. Stone photo courtesy of Martha Stewart.

Page 73, ARCO Forum crowd photo courtesy of Betty Donahue.

Page 74, Jonathan Moore and Nicholas Mitropoulos photo courtesy of Martha Stewart.

Page 75, Kennedy School staff photo courtesy of Dev Kernan; Mary Jo Bane photo courtesy of Martha Stewart.

Page 76, McCloy Scholar program photo courtesy of Daisy Agee.

Page 78, Edith Stokey photo courtesy of Martha Stewart; Derek Bok and Mary O'Keeffe photo courtesy of Martha Stewart; Helen "Sunny" Ladd and Herman "Dutch" Leonard photo courtesy of Martha Stewart; Mark Moore photo courtesy of Daisy Agee.

Page 80, Faculty photo courtesy of
Elizabeth Craig.

Page 81, Talent show photo courtesy of
Susan Lapides; volleyball photo courtesy
of Daisy Agee; jogging photo courtesy of
Martha Stewart.

Page 82, Executive program planners photo
courtesy of Daisy Agee.

Page 83, Hale Champion photo courtesy of
Sandra Johnson; Edwin Meese photo
courtesy of Martha Stewart.

Page 84, Paul M. Doty photo courtesy of
Susan Lapides.

Page 85, Coauthors of *Hawks, Doves, and
Owls* photo courtesy of Martha Stewart.

Page 86, Harvey Brooks photo courtesy of
Joe Wrinn; William W. Hogan photo
courtesy of Martha Stewart.

Page 88, Belfer Center "before" photo

courtesy of Susan Lapides, Belfer Center
"during" photo courtesy of Martha
Stewart.

Page 89, Belfer Center "after" photo
courtesy of Martha Stewart; groundbreaking ceremony photo courtesy of
Martha Stewart.

Page 90, Frank Weil and Winthrop Knowlton photo courtesy of Martha Stewart.

Page 91, Manuel Carballo photo courtesy
of Martha Stewart.

Page 92, Elliot Richardson photo courtesy
of E. Craig; Frank Stanton and Graham
Allison photo courtesy of Martha
Stewart.

Page 93, Washington debate photo courtesy
of Leslie Carno.

Page 94, Courtyard photo courtesy of
Michael Nagy.

INDEX

Abbreviations

HARVARD UNIVERSITY

CFIA	Center for International Affairs
FAS	Faculty of Arts and Sciences
GSD	Graduate School of Design
HBS	Harvard Business School
HGSE	Harvard Graduate School of Education
HIID	Harvard Institute for International Development
HLS	Harvard Law School
HMS	Harvard Medical School
SPH	School of Public Health

JOHN F. KENNEDY SCHOOL OF GOVERNMENT

CBG	Center for Business and Government
CHPM	Center for Health Policy and Management
CSIA	Center for Science and International Affairs
EEPC	Energy and Environmental Policy Center
IOP	Institute of Politics

KENNEDY SCHOOL FACULTY, 1936-1986

Alden, Vernon Roger
  *Assoc. Dean, Faculty of Business
    Administration*
  1961–1962
Allison, Graham Tillett, Jr.
  Don K. Price Prof. of Politics
  1969–
  Dean
  1977–
Alm, Alvin L.
  Adjunct Lecturer in Public Policy
  1981–1983
Andrews, Kenneth Richmond
  *Donald K. David Prof. of Business
    Administration*
  1972–1975
Apgar, William C.
  *Assoc. Prof. of City and Regional
    Planning*
  1980–
Applebaum, Noha
  Lecturer in City and Regional Planning
  1980–1984
  Senior Preceptor in Writing,
  1982–
Areeda, Phillip Elias
  Prof. of Law
  1967–1974
Arrow, Kenneth J.
  James Bryant Conant University Prof.
  1973–1975
Bailey, Stephen K.
  *Francis Keppel Prof. of Educational
    Policy and Administration (HGSE)*
  1980–1982
Baker, George Pierce
  James J. Hill Prof. of Transportation
  1950–1954

Baldwin, Robert Edward
  Asst. Prof. of Economics
  1955–1957
Bambach, Dorothy
  *Asst. Dean; Director, Master of Public
    Policy Program*
  1978–1981
Bane, Mary Jo
  Prof. of Public Policy
  1981–
Banfield, Edward Christie
  *Henry Lee Shattuck Prof. of Urban
    Government*
  1959–1972
Barringer, Richard Edward
  Lecturer on Public Policy
  1970–1972
  Asst. Dean
  1970–1971
Barzelay, Michael
  Asst. Prof. of Public Policy
  1985–
Bator, Francis M.
  Prof. of Political Economy
  1967–
Beatty, John Francis
  Lecturer on Public Administration
  1971–1972
Beer, Samuel Hutchison
  *Eaton Prof. of the Science of
    Government (FAS)*
  1954–1982
Behn, Robert D.
  Vis. Assoc. Prof. (Duke University)
  1985–
Bell, David Elliott
  Lecturer on Economics; Secretary
  1959–1961

Bergson, Abram
  George F. Baker Prof. of Economics
  1968–1974
Berry, Ralph Edward
  Assoc. Prof. of Economics (SPH)
  1966–1975
Bevis, Howard Landis
  *Wm. Ziegler Prof. of Government and
    Law*
  1937–1939
Bhatia, Ramesh
  *Visiting Assoc. Prof. of City and
    Regional Planning*
  1980–1981
Black, Donald
  Lecturer of Law and Sociology (HLS)
  1981–1982
Black, John Donald
  Henry Lee Prof. of Economics
  1937–1956
Blackwill, Robert D.
  *Lecturer in Public Policy;
    Assoc. Dean for Administration*
  1983–1985
Bloom, Howard S.
  *Assoc. Prof. of City and Regional
    Planning*
  1975–1977; 1980–
Blumenthal, David
  *Lecturer in Public Policy; Exec. Director,
    CHPM*
  1983–
Boersch-Supan, Axel
  Asst. Prof. of Public Policy
  1984–
Bok, Derek Curtis
  Prof. of Law (HLS)
  1965–

President
1971–
Bok, Sissela
  Lecturer on Medical Ethics (HMS)
  1980–1985
Bookstein, Fred L.
  Lecturer on Public Administration
  1971–1972
Bower, Joseph Lyon
  Prof. of Business Administration (HBS)
  1969–
Bowie, Robert Richardson
  *Clarence Dillon Prof. of International
    Affairs*
  1952–1954; 1957–1977
Brewster, Kingman, Jr.
  Prof. of Law
  1959–1960
Breyer, Stephen Gerald
  Lecturer on Law (HLS)
  1971–1974; 1977–1981; 1982–
Brinser, Ayers
  *Lecturer on Natural Resources
    Management and Development at the
    Harvard Forest*
  1952–1960
Broadman, Harry G.
  *Adjunct Lecturer in Public Policy
    (EEPC)*
  1985–
Broadnax, Walter D.
  Lecturer in Public Policy
  1981–
Brock, Jonathan
  Lecturer in Public Policy
  1980–1982
Brooks, Harvey
  Benjamin Peirce Prof. of Technology and

Public Policy; Prof. of Applied Physics
1962–
Brown, H. James
  Prof. of City and Regional Planning
  1973–1975
  *Director, State, Local, and
    Intergovernmental Center*
  1980–
Brown, John Poole, Jr.
  Asst. Dean and Director of Admissions
  1976–1977
Bruner, Jerome Seymour
  Prof. of Psychology
  1948–1953; 1960–1962
Bruning, Heinrich
  Lucius N. Littauer Prof. of Government
  1938–1952
Brzezinski, Zbigniew
  Asst. Prof. of Government
  1956–1960
Buck, Paul Herman
  Provost of the University
  1949–1953
Bundy, McGeorge
  Prof. of Government
  1952–1961
Bupp, Irvin Carney, Jr.
  Lecturer on Public Administration
  1971–1973
Burbank, Harold Hitchings
  *David A. Wells Prof. of Political
    Economy*
  1937–1951
Butters, John Keith
  Prof. of Business Administration
  1951–1958
Capron, William Mosher
  Senior Lecturer on Political Economy

1969–1977
Assoc. Dean
1969–1978
Carballo, Manuel
Lecturer in Public Policy
1978–1979; 1980–1983
Carnesale, Albert
Prof. of Public Policy
1982–
Academic Dean
1977–
Carter, Ashton B.
Asst. Prof. of Public Policy
Asst. Director, CSIA
1984–
Cavers, David Farquhar
Prof. of Law
1950–1951
Caves, Richard Earl
Galen Stone Prof. of International Trade
1962–1975
Champion, Hale
Executive Dean
1972–1975; 1980–
Chase, Gordon
Lecturer in Public Policy
1974–1975; 1976–1979
Chayes, Abram
Felix Frankfurter Prof. of Law (HLS)
1985–
Chayes, Antonia H.
Adjunct Lecturer in Public Policy
1981–
Chenery, Hollis Burnley
Thomas D. Cabot Prof. of Economics
(FAS)
1965–1972; 1973–1974; 1975–1979;
1983–

Cherington, Charles Richards
Prof. of Government
1946–1966
Secretary
1946–1951
Acting Dean
1951–1952
Cherington, Paul Whiton
James J. Hill Prof. of Transportation
1951–1954; 1965–1969
Christensen, C. Roland
George Fisher Baker, Jr. Prof. of Business
Administration
1974–1975
Christenson, Charles John
Jesse Isidor Straus Prof. of Business
Administration (HBS)
1973–
Clark, Gordon L.
Asst. Prof. of City and Regional
Planning
1980–1983
Cohen, I. Bernard
Victor S. Thomas Prof. of the History of
Science (FAS)
1960–1976; 1977–1978; 1979–1984
Cohen, Linda R.
Asst. Prof. of Public Policy
1978–1982
Conant, James Bryant
President
1937–1953
Conrad, Robert F.
Lecturer in Economics
1982–1983
Cooney, James A.
Adjunct Lecturer in Public Policy;
Exec. Director, McCloy Scholars

Program
1984–
Cooper, Joseph
Asst. Prof. of Government
1965–1967
Costle, Douglas M.
Adjunct Lecturer in Public Policy
1981–1982
Cox, Archibald
Royall Prof. of Law
1950–1956; 1960–1961
Crozier, Michael
Vis. Prof. of Sociology and Public
Administration
1966–1967; 1969–1970; 1979–1980
Cummings, Milton Curtis
Vis. Lecturer, Dept. of Government
(Johns Hopkins)
1967–1968
Daniels, Belden H.
Adjunct Lecturer in City and Regional
Planning
1980–1981
Daniere, Andre Lucien
Lecturer on Education and Economics
1964–1966
Darman, Richard Gordon
Lecturer in Public Policy
and Management
1977–1983
DeMuth, Christopher Clay
Lecturer in Public Policy; Director,
Harvard Faculty Project on
Regulation
1977–1982
Deutsch, Karl Wolfgang
Stanfield Prof. of International Peace
1967–1975

Devarajan, Shantayanan
  Assoc. Prof. of Public Policy
  1980–
Doebele, William A., Jr.
  Prof. of Advanced Environmental
    Studies (GSD)
  1980–1982; 1985–
Doeringer, Peter Brantley
  Assoc. Prof. of Political Economy
  1972–1974
  Vis. Prof. of Economics
  1975–1976
Doolittle, Fred C.
  Assoc. Prof. of City and Regional
    Planning
  1980–1983
Dorfman, Robert
  David A. Wells Prof. of Political
    Economy
  1956–1975
Doty, Paul Mead
  Mallinckrodt Prof. of Biochemistry;
    Dir. Emeritus, CSIA
  1969–1975; 1977–
Duesenberry, James Stemble
  William Joseph Maier Prof. of Money
    and Banking (FAS)
  1957–
Dukakis, Michael S.
  Lecturer in Public Policy; Director,
    Intergovernmental Studies
  1979–1982
Dunlop, John Thomas
  Lamont University Prof.
  1943; 1946–1980
Dupre, J. Stefan
  Asst. Prof. of Government
  1961–1963

Secretary
  1961–1963
  Vis. Mackenzie King Prof. of
    Canadian Studies
  1978–1979
Ebert, Robert Higgins
  Caroline Shields Walker Prof. of
    Medicine Emeritus (HMS)
  1969–1975; 1978–1981
Eckstein, Otto
  Prof. of Economics
  1958–1975
Edley, Christopher E.
  Asst. Prof. of Law
    (HLS)
  1978–1979; 1981–
Eisenstadt, Samuel Noah
  Vis. Prof. of Sociology (Hebrew
    University Jerusalem)
  1968–1969
Eizenstat, Stuart E.
  Adjunct Lecturer in Public Policy
  1981–
Elliott, William Yandell
  Leroy B. Williams Prof. of History and
    Political Science
  1938–1963
Ellwood, David T.
  Assoc. Prof. of Public Policy
  1980–1981; 1982–
Emerson, Rupert
  Prof. of Government
  1948–1970
England, Mary Jane
  Asst. Dean and Director, Lucius N.
    Littauer Program in Public
    Administration
  1984–

Fainsod, Merle
  Carl H. Pforzheimer University Prof.
  1940; 1946–1972
Fair, Gordon Maskew
  Gordon McKay Prof. of Sanitary
    Engineering; Abbott and
    James Lawrence Prof. of Engineering
  1956–1961
Fairley, William Bishop
  Assoc. Prof. of Statistics
  1970–1976
Falcon, Walter Phillip
  Asst. Prof. of Economics
  1966–1967
Fauth, Gary R.
  Assoc. Prof. of City and Regional
    Planning
  1980–1984
Fayde, Reese W.
  Adjunct Lecturer in Public Policy
  1981–1982
Fein, Rashi
  Prof. of the Economics of Medicine
  1968–1975
Feldman, Penny Hollander
  Lecturer on Political Science
    (SPH)
  1978–
Feldstein, Martin Stuart
  Prof. of Economics
  1967–1975
Fenn, Dan Huntington, Jr.
  Lecturer on Business Administration
    (HBS)
  1972–1975; 1981–
Ferguson, Ronald F.
  Asst. Prof. of Public Policy
  1983–

Fineberg, Harvey Vernon
  Asst. Prof. of Health Services
  Administration (SPH)
  1974–1979; 1980–1982
Flanagan, Stephen J.
  Executive Director, CSIA
  1985–
Fleck, James D.
  Vis. Mackenzie King Prof. of
  Canadian Studies
  1978–1979
Ford, Franklin Lewis
  McLean Prof. of Ancient and Modern
  History
  1964–1974
Ford, James
  Assoc. Prof. of Social Ethics
  1943
Fox, Daniel Michael
  Asst. Prof. of History
  1969–1971
Frank, Barney
  Adjunct Lecturer in Public Policy
  1977–1981
Freidel, Frank Burt, Jr.
  Charles Warren Prof. of American
  History
  1972–1975
Friedrich, Carl J.
  Eaton Prof. of the Science of
  Government
  1937–1971
Galbraith, John Kenneth
  Paul M. Warburg Prof. of Economics
  1938; 1949–1975
Ganley, Oswald H.
  Adjunct Lecturer in Public Policy
  1983–

Gansler, Jacques
  Adjunct Lecturer in Public Policy
  1984–
Garwin, Richard L.
  Prof. of Public Policy
  1979–1981
Gaus, John Merriman
  Prof. of Government
  1941–1942; 1947–1961
Gifford, Bernard Robert
  Adjunct Lecturer in Public Policy
  1977–1978
Goldman, Guido Graham
  Senior Lecturer on Government (FAS);
  Chairman, McCloy Scholars Program;
  Advisor to the Kennedy Memorial
  German Fellows
  1973–
Goldwin, Robert A.
  Adjunct Lecturer in Public Policy
  1983–1984
Gomez-Ibanez, José A.
  Prof. of Public Policy and Urban
  Planning
  1980–
Gordon, Lester Elliott
  Director, HIID
  1972–1975
Gordon, Lincoln
  William Ziegler Prof. of International
  Relations
  1946–1951; 1959–1963
Gordon, Richard S.
  Adjunct Lecturer in Public Policy
  1977–1978
Gourevitch, Peter Alexis
  Asst. Prof. of Government
  1971–1973

Gray, Clive Studley
  Lecturer in Economics
  1978–1980
Green, Jerry
  Prof. of Economics (FAS)
  1984–
Griliches, Zvi
  Nathaniel Ropes Prof. of Political
  Economy; Chairman, Dept. of
  Economics
  1980–1983
Griswold, Erwin Nathaniel
  Prof. of Law
  1937–1940
Gross, Leo
  Vis. Prof. of Government
  1969–1972
Gustafson, Thane Eric
  Asst. Prof. of Government
  1975–1979
Haar, Charles Monroe
  Louis D. Brandeis Prof. of Law
  1960–1968; 1969–1975
Haberler, Gottfried
  Galen L. Stone Prof. of International
  Trade
  1940–1971
Hamburg, David Alan
  John D. MacArthur Foundation
  Prof. of Health Policy and
  Management; Director, CHPM
  1979–1983
Hamilton, Margaret
  Asst. Dean and Registrar
  1981–1983
Hamlin, Robert Henry
  Robert Irving Lee Prof. of Public Health
  1961–1966

Hansen, Alvin Harvey
  *Lucius N. Littauer Prof. of Political
    Economy*
  1937–1956
Harris, Seymour Edwin
  *Lucius N. Littauer Prof. of Political
    Economy*
  1940–1964
Harrison, David, Jr.
  *Assoc. Prof. of City and Regional
    Planning*
  1980–1985
Hart, Henry Melvin
  Prof. of Law
  1940–1941
Hartz, Louis
  Prof. of Government
  1954–1966; 1967–1975
Heclo, Hugh H.
  Prof. of Government (FAS)
  1980–
Heifetz, Ronald L.
  Lecturer in Public Policy
  1984–
Heimert, Alan Edward
  *Powell M. Cabot Prof. of American
    Literature*
  1972–1975
Herring, Edward Pendleton
  Asst. Prof. of Government; Secretary
  1937–1946
Herzlinger, Regina E.
  *Assoc. Prof. of Business
    Administration*
  1977–1978
Herzog, Paul M.
  Assoc. Dean
  1954–1957

Heymann, Philip Benjamin
  Prof. of Law
  1970–1980; 1981–
Hirschman, Albert Otto
  *Lucius N. Littauer Prof. of Political
    Economy*
  1964–1974
Hitchner, Stephen Ballinger
  Instructor in Public Policy
  1974–1978
Hoffmann, Stanley Harry
  Prof. of Government
  1961–1975
Hofheinz, Roy Mark
  Prof. of Government
  1972–1975
Hogan, William W.
  *Prof. of Political Economy;
    Director, EEPC; Chairman,
    Public Policy Program*
  1978–
Holcombe, Arthur Norman
  Prof. of Government
  1937–1955
Howitt, Arnold M.
  *Assoc. Prof. of City and Regional
    Planning*
  1980–1983
Hubbard, R. Glenn
  *Vis. Asst. Prof. (Northwestern
    University)*
  1985–
Huntington, Samuel Phillips
  Frank G. Thomson Prof. of Government
  1963–1975
Ingram, Gregory Keith
  Asst. Prof. of Economics
  1973–1975

Irving, Frederick
  *Asst. Dean and Director of Career
    Development*
  1979–1980
Isaacs, Nathan
  Prof. of Business Law
  1937–1941
Jackson, Ira Abbott
  Assoc. Dean
  1976–1983
Jackson, John Edgar
  Asst. Prof. of Government
  1970–1975
Jacoby, Henry Donnan
  Assoc. Prof. of Political Economy
  1967–1973
Jaffe, Louis Leventhal
  Byrne Prof. of Administrative Law
  1951–1954; 1961–1965
Jenkins, Glenn P.
  Lecturer on Public Policy
  1985–
Johnson, Kenneth Lewis
  Adjunct Lecturer in Public Policy
  1977–1978
Jorgenson, Dale
  *Frederick Eaton Abbe Prof. of
    Economics (FAS)*
  1984–
Kain, John Forrest
  Prof. of Economics
  1965–1975
  Prof. of City and Regional Planning
  1980–
Katz, Milton
  *Byrne Prof. of Administrative
    Law*
  1939–1940; 1948–1951

Katzenbach, Edward Lawrence, Jr.
  Director Harvard Defense Studies
    Program
  1956–1957
Kaufmann, William W.
  Lecturer on Public Policy
  1984–
Kaysen, Carl
  Lucius N. Littauer Prof. of Political
    Economy
  1951–1966; 1967–1970
  Assoc. Dean
  1961–1966
Kearns, Doris Helen
  Assoc. Prof. of Government
  1969–1975
Kelling, George L.
  Adjunct Lecturer in Public Policy
  1983–
Kelman, Steven Jay
  Assoc. Prof. of Public Policy
  1978–
Kennedy, Maynard Thomas
  Prof. of Business Administration
  1965–1968
Keppel, Francis
  Dean, Faculty of Education
  1961–1963
Kerr, Andrew
  Assoc. Lecturer
  1975–1977
Key, V.O.
  Jonathan Trumbull Prof. of American
    History and Government
  1951–1964
Kiley, Robert Raymond
  Adjunct Lecturer in Public Policy
  1977–1978

Kilson, Martin Luther
  Prof. of Government
  1970–1975
Kissinger, Henry Alfred
  Prof. of Government; Assoc. Director
    CFIA; Director Defense Studies
    Program
  1958–1969
Kistiakowsky, George Bogdan
  Abbot and James Lawrence Prof. of
    Chemistry
  1967–1971
Klitgaard, Robert Emery
  Assoc. Prof. of Public Policy
  1977–1984
Knowlton, Winthrop
  Henry R. Luce Prof. of Ethics;
    Director, CBG
  1983–
Kresge, David T.
  Adjunct Lecturer in Public Policy;
    Director, Joint Center for Urban
    Studies
  1981–1982
Kristol, William
  Asst. Prof. of Public Policy
  1983–
Kuechle, David
  Prof. of Education
    (HGSE)
  1980–
Kurth, James Ransom
  Asst. Prof. of Government
  1969–1971
Ladd, Helen G.
  Assoc. Prof. of City and Regional
    Planning
  1980–

Lambie, Morris Bryan
  Prof. of Government
  1937–1954
Leach, Walter Barton
  Story Prof. of Law
  1954–1969
Lee, Henry
  Adjunct Lecturer in Public Policy;
    Exec. Director,
    EEPC
  1983–
Lee, Sidney Seymour
  Clinical Prof. of Hospital Care and
    Medical Care Administration; Assoc.
    Dean, Faculty of Medicine
  1970–1972
Leigh, Wilhelmina A.
  Asst. Prof. of City and Regional
    Planning
  1980–1982
Leonard, Herman Beukema
  Assoc. Prof. of Public Policy
  1979–
Leone, Robert A.
  Lecturer in Public Policy
  1982–
Liebman, Lance Malcolm
  Asst. Prof. of Law
  1971–1974
Light, Richard Jay
  Prof. of Education
  1973–
Linsky, Martin A.
  Lecturer in Public Policy
  1981–
Lipset, Seymour Martin
  Prof. of Government
  1965–1975

Livernash, Edward Robert
Prof. of Business Administration
1961–1964
Lombard, James M.
Asst. Dean and Registrar
1974–1976
Loury, Glenn C.
Prof. of Political Economy; Prof. of
Afro-American Studies
1984–
Lucker, Marjorie
Asst. Dean and Registrar
1983–
Lukas, J. Anthony
Adjunct Lecturer
1979–1982
Lupu, Nancy Altman
Lecturer in Public Policy
1983–
Lynn, Laurence Edwin, Jr.
Prof. of Public Policy
1974–1983
Chairman, Public Policy Program
1978–
Maass, Arthur A.
Prof. of Government
1951–1984
Maier, Charles Steven
Asst. Prof. of History
1969–1972;
1973–1974
Majone, Giandomenico
Vis. Prof.
(University of Calabria)
1985–
Manley, Gertrude
Registrar
1953–1973

Mann, Lawrence Dale
Prof. of City Planning
1972–1975
Manne, Alan Sussman
Prof. of Political Economy
1974–1976
Manning, Willard G.
Asst. Prof. of Public Policy
1973–1975
Mansfield, Harvey Claflin
Prof. of Government; Chairman,
Dept. of Government
1973–1977
Marchant, Edward H.
Adjunct Lecturer in City and Regional
Planning
1980–
Marglin, Stephen Alan
Asst. Prof. of Economics
1965–1968
Markham, Jesse
Vis. Prof., HBS (Princeton)
1965–1966
Martin, Samuel Preston
Vis. Prof. of Preventive Medicine
1969–1970
Mason, Bayley
Assoc. Dean for Alumni Affairs and
Development
1980–
Mason, Edward S.
Lamont University Prof.
1947–1958
Dean
1938–1969
May, Ernest R.
Charles Warren Prof.
of History;

Chairman, Ph.D. Program
1967–
McCloskey, Robert Green
Jonathan Trumbull Prof. of American
History and Government
1950–1970
McKean, Roland Neely
Vis. Prof. of Economics and Education
(UCLA)
1966–1967
Mechling, Jerry
Adjunct Lecturer in Public Policy
1984–
Memishian, Pamela Ann
Lecturer on Public Administration
1975–1976
Merriam, Charles E.
Vis. Lecturer on Government
1940
Meselson, Matthew S.
Thomas Dudley Cabot Prof. of the
Natural Sciences (FAS)
1983–
Mesthene, Emmanuel George
Lecturer on Business Administration
1966–1972
Exec. Director, Harvard University
Program on Technology and Society
1973–1974
Meyer, Albert Julius
Assoc. Prof. of Middle Eastern Studies;
Lecturer on Economics
1960–1975
Meyer, John R.
James W. Harpel Prof. of Capital
Formation and Economic Growth
1960–1968;
1973–

Michelman, Frank Isaac
  Prof. of Law
  1970–1974
Mills, Daniel Quinn
  Assoc. Prof. of Industrial Relations
  (M.I.T.)
  1973–1975
Montgomery, John D.
  Prof. of Public Administration;
  Secretary
  1963–
Moore, Jonathan
  Lecturer in Public Policy; Director,
  Institute of Politics
  1974–
Moore, Mark H.
  Daniel and Florence Guggenheim Prof.
  of Criminal Justice Policy and
  Management
  1972–
Mosley, Calvin N.
  Asst. Dean; Exec. Director, Program in
  Public Policy
  1981–
Mosteller, Charles Frederick
  Roger Irving Lee Prof. of Mathematical
  Statistics
  1969–
Moynihan, Daniel Patrick
  Prof. of Government
  1966–1969; 1970–1975
Mundel, David Steven
  Assoc. Prof. of Public Policy
  1972–1977
Murray, Robert J.
  Lecturer in Public Policy; Director,
  National Security Programs
  1984–

Musgrave, Richard Abel
  Harold Hitchings Burbank Prof. of
  Political Economy; Prof. of Economics
  (HLS)
  1965–1975
Nachmias, David
  Lecturer in the Summer Seminar in
  Quantitative Analysis
  1976–1977
Nacht, Michael
  Assoc. Prof. of Public Policy;
  Assoc. Director, CSIA
  1977–1984
Natchez, Peter Ben
  Lecturer on Public Administration
  1971–1972
Nelson, Valerie Irene
  Lecturer in Public Policy
  1974–1979
Neustadt, Richard Elliott
  Lucius N. Littauer Prof. of Public
  Administration
  1965–
  Assoc. Dean
  1965–1975
  Director, IOP
  1967–1974
Nichols, Albert L.
  Assoc. Prof. of Public Policy
  1976–
Nosanchuk, Terrance Aaron
  Vis. Lecturer on Statistics
  1969–1970
Nye, Joseph S.
  Clarence Dillon Prof. of International
  Affairs
  1966–1975;
  1979–

  Director, CSIA
  1985–
O'Hare, Michael
  Lecturer in Public Policy
  1981–
O'Keeffe, Mary M.
  Asst. Prof. of Public Policy
  1981–
O'Neil, William A.
  Asst. Dean for Financial Affairs
  1977–
Oettinger, Anthony Gervin
  Gordon McKay Prof. of Applied
  Mathematics; Prof. of Information
  Resources (FAS)
  1973–
Oldman, Oliver
  Prof. of Law
  1967–1975
Orren, Gary R.
  Assoc. Prof. of Public Policy
  1971–1972; 1975–1977;
  1980–
Oye, Kenneth Akito
  Lecturer on Public Administration
  1975–1977
Papanek, Gustav Fritz
  Lecturer on Economics
  1966–1974
Peretz, Martin H.
  Lecturer on Social Studies
  1973–1975
Perkins, Dwight Heald
  Prof. of Modern China Studies
  1965–1966
  Director, HIID
  1970–1975;
  1977–

Peterson, Osler Luther
  Prof. of Preventive Medicine
  1961–1975
Pickrell, Don H.
  *Asst. Prof. of City and Regional
  Planning*
  1980–1985
Pitfield, P. Michael
  *William Lyon MacKenzie King Vis. Prof.
  of Canadian Studies*
  1980–1981
Pizzorno, Alessandro Degiovanni
  *Vis. Prof. of Sociology (Urbino
  University Italy)*
  1968–1969
Polenske, Karen Rosel
  Instructor in Economics
  1966–1967
Porter, Roger
  Prof. of Government and Business
  1979–1983; 1985–
Price, Don K., Jr.
  *Weatherhead III and Richard W.
  Weatherhead Prof. of Public
  Management Emeritus*
  1958–
  Dean
  1958–1977
Price, Hugh Douglas
  Prof. of Government
  1966–1975
Prottas, Jeffrey Manditch
  *Assoc. Prof. of City and Regional
  Planning*
  1980–1983
Pusey, Nathan Marsh
  President
  1953–1971

Putnam, Robert
  Prof. of Government (FAS)
  1984–
Radner, Roy
  *Vis. Prof. of Economics and
  Statistics
  (UC Berkeley)*
  1978–1979
Raiffa, Howard
  *Frank Plumpton Ramsey Prof. of
  Managerial Economics*
  1966–
Raines, Franklin D.
  Adjunct Lecturer in Public Policy
  1980–
Rainwater, Lee
  Prof. of Sociology
  1969–1975
Raup, Hugh Miller
  *Prof. of Botany; Director of Harvard
  Forest*
  1958–1960
Ravitch, Richard
  Adjunct Lecturer in Public Policy
  1984–1985
Reich, Robert B.
  Lecturer in Public Policy
  1981–
Reischauer, Edwin Oldfather
  University Prof.
  1967–1974
Reiser, Stanley Joel
  Asst. Prof. of the History of Medicine
  1972–1975
Richmond, Julius B.
  *John D. MacArthur Prof. of Health
  Policy Management*
  1983–

Roberts, Marc Jeffrey
  *Prof. of Political Economy and Health
  Policy*
  1972–
Robyn, Dorothy L.
  Asst. Prof. of Public Policy
  1983-
Rodrik, Dani
  Asst. Prof. of Public Policy
  1985-
Roe, David B.
  Lecturer in Law (HLS)
  1983–1984
Roemer, Michael
  Lecturer in Economics (FAS)
  1983–1984
Rogers, Peter P.
  *Gordon McKay Prof. of Environmental
  Engineering; Prof. of City and
  Regional Planning*
  1980-
Rosenthal, Stephen R.
  Vis. Assoc. Prof. (Boston University)
  1982–1983
Rosenthal, Gerald David
  Asst. Prof. of Economics
  1966–1967
Rosovsky, Henry
  *Walter S. Barker Prof. of Economics
  (FAS)*
  1969–1984
Rowen, Henry Stanislaus
  Vis. Member, IOP
  1967-1969
Ruggles, Clyde Orval
  *Prof. of Public Utility Management and
  Regulation*
  1941–1950

Salter, Malcolm
Prof. of Business (HBS)
1985–

Sandberg, Lars Gunnarsson
Asst. Prof. of Economics
1966–1967

Sander, Frank Ernest Arnold
Prof. of Law
1963–1975

Sato, Ryuzo
Adjunct Prof. of Public Policy (Brown University)
1983–

Schelling, Thomas C.
Lucius N. Littauer Prof. of Political Economy; Director, Institute for the Study of Smoking Behavior and Policy
1960–

Schneider, William
Lecturer on Public Administration
1971–1972

Schydlowsky, Daniel Moses
Asst. Prof. of Economics
1967–1972

Sebenius, James K.
Assoc. Prof. of Public Policy
1980–

Shapiro, Michael H.
Assoc. Prof. of City and Regional Planning
1980–1983

Shapiro, Martin M.
Prof. of Government
1971–1974

Shemo, Thomas Edward
Lecturer in the Summer Seminar in Quantitative Analysis
1976–1977

Shepard, Ward
Director of Harvard Forest
1937–1938

Shklar Judith Nisse
Prof. of Government
1966–1975

Sizer, Theodore Ryland
Dean, Faculty of Education
1964–1969

Slichter, Sumner Huber
Lamont University Professor
1937–1960

Smith, Dan Throop
Prof. of Finance
1944–1956; 1960–1969

Smith, Norman R.
Asst. Dean; Director, Career, Alumni, and Student Services
1981–1984

Smithies, Arthur
Nathaniel Ropes Prof. of Political Economy
1950–1957;
1958–1978

Smoke, Richard Leroy
Lecturer on Pubic Policy; Asst. Dean
1971–1973

Solow, Robert Merton
Prof. of Economics (M.I.T.)
1969–1974

Spence, Michael
George Gund Prof. of Economics and Business Administration (FAS and HBS)
1972–1973
Dean of FAS
1983–

Steinbruner, John David
Assoc. Prof. of Public Policy
1969–1976

Stern, Joseph J.
Lecturer on Economics (FAS)
1981–1985

Stevens, Carl
Vis. Prof. of Economics (Reed College)
1966–1967

Stewart, Richard Burleson
Prof. of Law (HLS)
1977–

Stock, James H.
Asst. Prof. of Public Policy
1984–

Stokey, Edith Morton
Lecturer in Public Policy; Secretary of the School
1974–

Stoto, Michael A.
Assoc. Prof. of Public Policy
1979–

Straszheim, Mahlon Reid
Asst. Prof. of Economics
1970–1971

Surrey, Stanley Sterling
Jeremiah Smith, Jr., Prof. of Law
1951–1961;
1969–1975

Sutherland, Arthur Eugene
Bussey Prof. of Law; Vis. Lecturer in Dept. of Government
1950–1969

Tarver, Leon R., Jr.
Asst. Dean and Director, Public Administration Program
1979–1980

Thomas, Carol J.
Adjunct Lecturer in City and Regional
Planning
1980–1981; 1982–1983
Thomas, Harold Allen, Jr.
Gordon McKay Prof. of Civil and
Sanitary Engineering
1956–1974
Thomas, John W.
Lecturer in Public Policy
1982–
Thompson, Mark Smith
Asst. Prof. of Health Services (SPH)
1976–1978
Thurow, Lester Carl
Prof. of Management and Economics
(M.I.T.)
1969–1970; 1971–1975
Timmer, C. Peter
John D. Black Prof. of Agriculture and
Business (HBS)
1981–
Tomey, Edward J.
Adjunct Lecturer in City and Regional
Planning
1980–1981
Treverton, Gregory F.
Lecturer in Public Policy
1981–
Trueheart, William E.
Asst. Dean and Director of the Lucius
N. Littauer Program in Public
Administration
1980–1984
Tufte, Edward Rolf
Lecturer in Summer Seminar in
Quantitative Analysis
1976–1977

Turner, Donald Frank
Prof. of Law
1959–1965
Ulam, Adam Bruno
Prof. of Government
1960–1975
Ullman, Richard Henry
Asst. Prof. of Government
1963–1965
Van der Heyden, Ludo
Asst. Prof. of Public Policy
1978–1980
Vaupel, James Walton
Lecturer on Public
Administration
1973–1974
Verba, Sidney
Prof. of Government; Chairman, Dept.
of Government
1977–1980
Verdier, James M.
Lecturer in Public Policy
1983–
Vernon Raymond
Clarence F. Dillon Prof. of International
Affairs Emeritus
1960–1975;
1978–
Vidal, Avis C.
Assoc. Prof. of City and Regional
Planning
1980–
Viscusi, William Gregory
Instructor in Public Policy
1974–1976
Wallace, Donald Holmes
Asst. Prof. of Economics
1938–1939

Walzer, Michael Laban
Prof. of Government
1971–1974
Warwick, Donald Philip
Lecturer on Social Relations
1967–1968; 1969–1971
Weiner, Harry
Lecturer in Public Administration
1970–1975
Asst. Dean and Registrar
1970–1974
Weinreb, Lloyd Lobell
Prof. of Law
1973–1975
Weinstein, Milton Charles
Prof. of Policy and Decision Sciences (SPH)
1973–
Wexler, Anne
Adjunct Lecturer in Public Policy
1981–1984
Willemain Thomas Reed
Assoc. Prof. of Public Policy
1979–1984
Willett, Thomas Dunaway
Asst. Prof. of Economics
1970–1971
Williams, John Henry
Nathaniel Ropes Prof. of
Political Economy
1937–1957
Dean
1937–1947
Williamson, Samuel Ruthven
Asst. Prof. of History
1971–1972
Wilson, Edwin Bidwell
Prof. of Vital Statistics
1937–1944

Wilson, James Q.
  *Henry Lee Shattuck Prof. of
    Government (FAS)*
  1961–1975; 1976–
Wilson, Julie Boatwright
  *Asst. Prof. of City and Regional
    Planning*
  1980–
Winokur, Herbert Simon
  Assoc. Lecturer
  1976–1977
Wise, David A.
  *John F. Stambaugh Prof. of Political
    Economy*
  1973–
Wofford, John Gardner
  *Research Associate in the Law School;
    Assoc. Director of IOP*
  1967–1969
Wolfson, Lewis W.
  Adjunct Lecturer in Public Policy
  1983–1984
Wood, Robert Coldwell
  Asst. Prof. of Government
  1956–1957; 1969–1970
Wortham, Anne
  Asst. Prof. of Public Policy
  1983–1985
Wright, Benjamin Fletcher
  Assoc. Prof. of Government
  1944–1948; 1966–1967
Wyatt, Joe Billy
  *Senior Lecturer (Division of Applied
    Science); University Vice President*

  for Administration
  1976–1983
Yaffee, Steven L.
  *Asst. Prof. of City and Regional
    Planning*
  1980–1983
Yarmolinsky, Adam
  Prof. of Law
  1967–1972
Yerby, Alonzo Smythe
  *Prof. of Health Services Administration;
    Assoc. Dean, Faculty of Public Health*
  1970–1975
Yergin, Daniel
  Adjunct Lecturer in Public Policy
  1979–1984
Yinger, John McHenry
  *Assoc. Prof. of City and Regional
    Planning*
  1980–
Zeckhauser, Richard Jay
  *Prof. of Political Economy; Chairman,
    Research Committee; Director,
    Harvard Faculty Project on
    Regulation*
  1969–
Zimmerman, Peter Brown
  *Asst. Dean and Director of Executive
    Training and Program Development*
  1977–
Zinberg, Dorothy Shore
  *Lecturer in Public Policy; Director of
    Seminars and Special Projects, CSIA*
  1979–

KENNEDY SCHOOL OFFICERS OF ADMINISTRATION, 1937–1986

President of the University

James Bryant Conant	1937–1953
Paul Herman Buck (Provost)	1949–1953
Nathan Marsh Pusey	1953–1971
Derek Curtis Bok	1971–

Dean of the Graduate School of Public Administration / John F. Kennedy School of Government

John Henry Williams	1937–1947
Edward Sagendorph Mason	1947–1958
Charles Richards Cherington (Acting Dean)	1951–1952
Don K. Price, Jr.	1958–1977
Graham Tillett Allison, Jr.	1977–

Secretary of the School

Edward Pendleton Herring	1937–1946
Charles Richards Cherington	1946–1951
Robert Green McCloskey	1950–1954
Arthur Aaron Maass	1954–1959
David Elliott Bell	1959–1961
J. Stefan Dupre	1961–1963
John Dickey Montgomery	1963–1977
Edith Morton Stokey	1977–

Associate or Senior Assistant Dean

Paul M. Herzog	1954–1957
Carl Kaysen	1961–1966
Richard Elliott Neustadt	1965–1975
William Mosher Capron	1969–1977
Ira Abbott Jackson	1977–1983
Bayley F. Mason	1980–
Robert D. Blackwill	1983–1985
Elizabeth Cairns Reveal	1985–

Academic Dean

Albert Carnesale	1982–

Executive Dean

Hale Champion	1980–

Registrar and Admissions Officer

Gertrude Manley	1953–1973
Harry Weiner	1973–1974
James Manuel Lombard	1974–1976
John Poole Brown, Jr.	1976–1977
Dorothy Bambach	1977–1981
Margaret Hamilton	1981–1983
Marjorie Lucker	1983–

Assistant Dean

Richard Edward Barringer	1970–1971
Richard Leroy Smoke	1971–1973
Harry Weiner	1970–1974
James Manuel Lombard	1974–1976
John Poole Brown, Jr.	1976–1977
Frederick Irving	1979–1980
Leon R. Tarver, Jr.	1979–1980
Dorothy Bambach	1978–1981
Margaret Hamilton	1981–1983
Norman R. Smith	1981–1984
William E. Truehart	1980–1984
William Augustus O'Neil	1977–
Peter Brown Zimmerman	1977–
Calvin N. Mosley	1981–
Marjorie Lucker	1983–
Mary Jane England	1984–